Descartes: A Very Short Introduction

VERY SHORT INTRODUCTIONS are for anyone wanting a stimulating and accessible way in to a new subject. They are written by experts, and have been published in more than 25 languages worldwide.

The series began in 1995, and now represents a wide variety of topics in history, philosophy, religion, science, and the humanities. Over the next few years it will grow to a library of around 200 volumes – a Very Short Introduction to everything from ancient Egypt and Indian philosophy to conceptual art and cosmology.

Very Short Introductions available now:

Available soon:

For more information visit our web site

www.oup.co.uk/vsi

Tom Sorell

DESCARTES

A Very Short Introduction

OXFORD
UNIVERSITY PRESS

For Alison

OXFORD
UNIVERSITY PRESS

Great Clarendon Street, Oxford OX2 6DP

Oxford University Press is a department of the University of Oxford.
It furthers the University's objective of excellence in research, scholarship,
and education by publishing worldwide in

Oxford New York

Auckland Bangkok Buenos Aires Cape Town Chennai
Dar es Salaam Delhi Hong Kong Istanbul Karachi Kolkata
Kuala Lumpur Madrid Melbourne Mexico City Mumbai Nairobi
São Paulo Shanghai Taipei Tokyo Toronto

Published in the United States
by Oxford University Press Inc., New York

© Tom Sorell 1987

The moral rights of the author have been asserted
Database right Oxford University Press (maker)

First published 1987 as an Oxford University Press paperback
Reissued 1996
First published as a Very Short Introduction 2000

British Library Cataloguing in Publication Data
Data available

Library of Congress Cataloging in Publication Data
Data available
ISBN 978-0-19-285409-4

15 17 19 20 18 16 14

Typeset by RefineCatch Ltd, Bungay, Suffolk
Printed in Great Britain by
Ashford Colour Press Ltd, Gosport, Hants.

Contents

Texts and Translations

References are made by volume and page number to the standard edition of Descartes's writings by Adam and Tannery (Paris: Vrin, 1964–75); '7. 12' means page 12 of volume 7 of Adam and Tannery. In general, translations are taken from J. Cottingham, R. Stoothoff, and D. Murdoch, *The Philosophical Writings of Descartes* (Cambridge: Cambridge University Press, 1985). Adam and Tannery volume numbers appear in this translation at the beginnings of works, Adam and Tannery page numbers in the margins. Volume numbers followed by 'A' refer to a Latin text, by 'B' to a French text. Extended quotations from Descartes's letters are taken from Anthony Kenny's translation and selection, *Descartes: Philosophical Letters* (Oxford: Oxford University Press, 1970).

List of Illustrations

The publisher and the author apologize for any errors or omissions in the above list. If contacted they will be pleased to rectify these at the earliest opportunity.

Chapter 1
Matter and Metaphysics

René Descartes had a short working life and it began late. He did not get down to sustained research in philosophy and the natural sciences until 1628, when he was thirty-two; it took him a further nine years to publish anything, and the last of his works to appear in his lifetime came out only twelve years after the first, in 1649. His output was not large. Yet he made fundamental contributions to physics, mathematics, and optics, and he reported useful observations in other fields, notably meteorology and physiology. Had he confined himself to the natural sciences his achievement would have been remarkable enough. But his range was in fact considerably wider.

He is best known, perhaps, as the man who said 'Cogito, ergo sum' – 'I am thinking, therefore I am'. This little piece of reasoning is the first principle of his metaphysics or first philosophy, his theory of what has to be known for stable and exact science to be possible at all. The metaphysical theory is extremely subtle, and its influence on philosophy down to the present day has been profound. Probably it is the most enduring of his intellectual achievements. But it was not intended to stand apart from his scientific work, let alone overshadow it. When Descartes turned to metaphysics at the beginning and towards the middle of his productive period, he developed a theory that was only supposed to clear the ground for the statement of his mathematical physics. By a complicated and very abstract argument, Descartes tried

1. Engraved portrait of Descartes from an original by Frans Hals

to prove that only properties well understood in geometry, namely length, depth, and breadth, were essential to matter, and that no properties but these geometrical ones and motion were needed to explain natural phenomena.

Descartes was not the only or the first advocate of geometrical physics. Galileo had pioneered the general approach, but in Descartes's opinion with insufficient rigour.' '[H]e has built without a foundation,' Descartes said of Galileo in a letter of October 1638.' '[W]ithout considering the primary cause of nature, he has sought only the reasons for some particular effects' (2. 380). Descartes's metaphysics considered the primary cause of nature – God; his physics deduced the causes of the most general phenomena of nature – such effects as acceleration and the deformation of bodies through collision – and put forward hypotheses about the causes of many others.

He was conscious of adopting a form of explanation that was very far removed from that of both common sense and traditional physics: it was not geared, as they were, to the appearances physical objects present to the human senses. Descartes's physics was constructed out of mathematical facts about material things, facts about size, shape, composition, and speed that could be grasped by a mind with sense-experience different from ours, or by a mind with no sense-experience at all. Other sorts of facts about physical objects, such as their having colour and smell – facts that *were* relative to the sensory powers of human beings – were dealt with differently. These Descartes explained in terms of the favoured framework of the sizes, shapes, and speeds of material things and their impacts on the sense-organs. The result was a theory that distinguished between properties that physical objects really and intrinsically possessed, such as shape and size, and properties that physical objects only appeared to possess, namely colour, smell, and other sensible qualities.

In distinguishing between a sense-based conception of the material world and the more austere, mathematical conception, Descartes committed himself to the view that the latter was the more objective of the two. Other believers in the new science were committed to the same thing. They sometimes tried to convey the superiority of the mathematical conception by saying that it was like God's. But Descartes was able to go beyond vague talk of a Godlike perspective and spell out the difference between the sense-based and mathematical conceptions of the material world. He showed that the former was systematically open to doubt while the latter was free of uncertainty, and he proposed a method for detaching oneself from the sense-based conception and adopting the more objective one.

Implementing the method himself, Descartes got impressive results in several branches of natural science as well as pure mathematics. Other writers, such as Francis Bacon and Galileo, were able to match his achievement only in part. Though Bacon developed a method for counteracting the limitations of common sense and traditional physics, his doubts about the sensory world were not as far-reaching as Descartes's. Again, while Bacon made room for a more objective conception of nature, he did not identify it as an essentially mathematical one. Galileo did make that identification but had no real theory to explain why the mathematical approach fitted the physical world so well. Cartesian metaphysics supplied the missing theory. It held that the human mind was constituted by God to enjoy perfect certainty about material things when conceiving them mathematically; it pointed out that God had the power to create whatever we could conceive with certainty; and it held that God was too benevolent to let the human mind fall into error when it conceived with certainty the mathematical nature of matter.

This explanation of how matter and mathematics were made for one another is not formulated in terms we are likely to find either familiar or compelling. But then we do not need to be persuaded that a mathematical physics is viable. The spectacular success of mathematical physics as an instrument of measurement, prediction, and control since the seventeenth century has made redundant any theory proving that a mathematical physics is possible. But the formulation of Descartes's theory helped to make way for some of the early research that produced the successes that have justified our confidence in the modern science of matter.

Descartes's metaphysical theory now commands more attention than his own particular version of mathematical physics, for his most distinctive speculations in the physical sciences started to be superseded within a few decades of his death. Nevertheless, the research that produced them and the process of assembling them virtually monopolized the productive period of his life. Scientific rather than philosophical questions dominated Descartes's work. He confronted them with a strong sense of what they had in common, with definite ideas about the order in which they should be tackled, and with the conviction that he personally could find answers to most of them.

Chapter 2
The Discovery of a Vocation

It seems to have been almost by accident that Descartes ever developed enough confidence in himself, or enough enthusiasm for the undertaking, to sustain the research programme he eventually began. When he was born in Touraine, in north-western France, on 31 March 1596, it was not into a family of scientists. His paternal grandfather and great-grandfather had both been doctors, but his father was a lawyer and magistrate. His maternal grandfather had held high public office in Poitiers. Other relations of his mother appear to have had jobs as legal officials. The families on both parents' sides were either minor aristocrats or on the fringes of the nobility, well off and well educated, but not particularly inclined towards science. Nothing in his early years at home pointed to his eventual career.

Probably at about the age of ten, the young René was sent to the Jesuit college of La Flèche in Anjou. Here he was a pupil for eight years, and received his early training in the sciences. In the last two years he was taught mathematics, for which he showed a special aptitude, and physics. It was not, however, the sort of physics that exploited mathematical results; Descartes was exposed to the scholastic theory of natural difference and change, a doctrine that purported to make sense of qualitatively described observations in obscure, abstract, and non-quantitative terms.

Among the Jesuits in the early 1600s the teaching of scholastic physics coexisted with an awareness of advances in astronomy that had been inspired by a quite different, mathematical approach to the investigation of nature. This was reflected at La Flèche. For instance, a celebration at the school in 1611 marked the discovery by Galileo of the moons of Jupiter. The Jesuits may even have been enlightened enough to make available newly invented optical instruments, on sale in Paris as early as 1609, to Descartes and his schoolfellows. But in the classroom stale scholastic doctrine seems to have predominated, and it bored Descartes. Or so he wrote later. In the quasi-autobiographical *Discourse on Method*, published in 1637 as the preface to three of his scientific essays, he gave the impression that he endured rather than profited from his schooldays. Only the mathematics he picked up at La Flèche helped him in later research, and even that, he claimed, had to be reworked in order to be serviceable. Apparently it was not at La Flèche in 1613 or 1614, but in Holland, five years later, that he first became interested in the sort of questions that dominated his published work.

Not much is known about what Descartes did between 1614, when he left La Flèche, and 1618, when he arrived in Holland. There is evidence that he took a law degree in Poitiers in 1616, his older brother Pierre having done so a few years before him. But while Pierre was launched by his father on a legal career, a military life seems to have been decided on for René. He went to Breda in Holland in 1618 and enlisted as a gentleman volunteer in the army of the Dutch Prince Maurice of Nassau. In effect he was an officer cadet in an army that doubled as military academy for young noblemen on the Continent.

In Breda, at the age of twenty-two, Descartes met a doctor some eight years older than himself called Isaac Beeckman. They became friends. Beeckman was a savant with a wide range of scientific interests, and his influence on the younger man was considerable. A letter of 1619 says as much. 'To tell you the truth,' Descartes wrote to Beeckman, 'it was really you who got me out of my idleness and made me remember things I once learnt and had nearly forgotten: when my mind wandered from serious matters, you put me back on the right path.' By 'serious matters' he seems to have meant a range of abstruse questions in pure and applied mathematics: the surviving letters between Descartes and Beeckman from this period speak of little else, and they seem to pick up where previous conversations between them had left off. One letter concerns mathematical relations between musical notes in songs for one voice; in another Descartes announces that he has found in six days solutions to four long-standing problems in mathematics. He also confided to Beeckman that he intended 'to give to the public a completely new science' for solving uniformly any arithmetical or geometrical problem whatever. It was at about this time, then, that Descartes's enthusiasm for scientific questions really began to take hold.

The correspondence with Beeckman started when Descartes left Breda for Copenhagen at the end of April 1619. Taking care to avoid the troop movements that were taking place owing to the outbreak of the Thirty Years War, he planned an extremely indirect route via Amsterdam and Danzig, then through Poland and eventually Austria and Bohemia. When he set off, as his letters show, he was very much preoccupied with mathematical questions. Instead of losing interest as his journey continued, he seems to have got more and more immersed in his reflections. Apparently he also changed his itinerary, for without having had the time to travel through Poland, Hungary, Austria, and Bohemia, he arrived in Frankfurt in September 1619, in time to be present for the coronation of the emperor Ferdinand.

He broke his journey for the winter in Germany, probably near Ulm. Here the researches he had been pursuing with such intensity may have become almost an obsession with him. In any case, on 10 November 1619, while shut away in a stove-heated room, he is supposed to have had a daytime vision and that night three dreams, which he took for divine revelation of his work in life – the unfolding of a *scientia mirabilis*, or wonderful science.

2. La Flèche. Seventeenth-century engraving by Pierre Aveline

Chapter 3
One Science, One Method

What Descartes saw in his daytime vision is unknown, and the account of his dreams in his private notebooks is so highly stylized and fragmentary that no reliable interpretation seems possible. Still, it is likely that what started to dawn on him was the unity under mathematics of a long list of sciences that had previously been regarded as distinct. The list included the four sciences traditionally put under the heading of the *quadrivium*, namely, arithmetic, geometry, music, and astronomy, as well as optics, mechanics, and some others.

A number of different sources suggest that after leaving Breda Descartes became increasingly receptive to the possibility of a master science, or a master method of scientific discovery. Writing to Beeckman from Amsterdam in April 1619, he describes meeting a savant who claimed to be able to employ a method from Raymond Lull's *Ars Parva* so successfully that he could hold forth for a whole hour on any subject at all. Lull was a thirteenth-century writer on universal science. Descartes took the claim seriously enough to ask Beeckman to look into the matter and advise him whether Lull's book was really so remarkable. Descartes himself had already written to Beeckman of his own vision of a science capable of unifying algebra and geometry, and this may have made him susceptible to the idea of a method adequate for making discoveries in, or speaking intelligently on, any subject whatever.

He looked beyond Lull for a master method, flirting for a time with

Rosicrucianism, which was rumoured to be a source of some kind of synoptic understanding. While living near Ulm he came into contact with a mathematician called Johann Faulhaber, who is known to have been a Rosicrucian, and who probably told Descartes something about the sect's secret beliefs. In later years, in order to deflect the accusation that he himself was a member of the outlawed brotherhood, Descartes said he had found nothing certain in its doctrines. But if he disowned the Rosicrucians, it was not immediately after meeting Faulhaber. Fragments from a notebook he kept after leaving Germany speak of a work in which he intended to lay down 'the means of solving all the difficulties in the science of mathematics . . . The work is offered afresh to learned men throughout the world and especially to the distinguished brothers of the Rose Croix in Germany' (10. 214).

The notebook I have just quoted from goes on to speak of an underlying unity in the sciences: 'If we could see how the sciences are linked together, we would find them no harder to retain in our minds than the series of numbers' (10. 215). It is unclear whether precisely this thought had occurred to him in the winter of 1619, but some related considerations – about the order in which the sciences should be studied – do appear to have been before his mind, if the account he gives in the *Discourse on Method* is to be believed.

Part Two of the *Discourse* gives a report of Descartes's reflections in the stove-heated room. He is supposed to have begun by considering that artefacts are less good when they are the creations of many people than when they are produced single-handed, and worse when they are developed *ad hoc* than when they are made according to a master plan. Still, it is sometimes better not to try to remake completely what has developed in a disorderly way. Just as no one would dream of tearing down and replacing *all* the houses in an unplanned city for the sake of achieving a more attractive overall effect, so, Descartes says, 'it would be unreasonable for an individual . . . to plan to reform the body of the sciences or the established order of teaching them in the schools'

(6. 13). On the other hand, it could well make sense for an individual to raze and rebuild his own particular house, and, by the same token, there might be something to be said for reforming ones's own learning – rejecting everything doubtful in ones's acquired beliefs – while leaving the body of the sciences and the established order of teaching them intact. One of the first conclusions Descartes reached, according to the *Discourse*, was that there would be nothing wrong with his getting rid of all his own – opinions and finding something better to replace them with – so long as he had worked out in advance a *method* of finding replacements (6. 17).

What Descartes looked for was a method that would have all the advantages but none of the drawbacks of the procedures followed in logic, algebra, and geometry. He claimed in the *Discourse* to have found such a method, and to have applied it with some success. 'In fact, I venture to say that by strictly observing the few rules I had chosen, I became very adept at unravelling all the questions which fall under [geometrical analysis and algebra]' (6. 20). A little later he says that, 'since I did not restrict the method to a subject matter, I hoped to apply it as successfully to the problems of the other sciences as I had to the problems of algebra' (6. 21). This is as close as Descartes comes in the *Discourse* to claiming that, while in Germany, he found a master method, a method that was applicable in principle to all scientific questions. He stops short of saying that the method actually *was* adequate for the other sciences. Instead, he reports thinking that since the principles of the other sciences all depended on philosophy, in which he found nothing certain, he had first to establish certainties in that field. What is more, he realized that this was not a task to be undertaken prematurely: 'I thought that I ought not to try to accomplish it until I had reached a more mature age than twenty-three, as I then was, and until I had first spent a long time in preparing myself for it' (6. 22). As we shall see, Descartes's 'preparations' lasted nine years. It was not until 1628 that he began establishing the 'certain principles' he thought were necessary for solving problems in the other sciences.

Chapter 4

'Absolutes', Simple Natures, and Problems

What method, if any, had Descartes discovered before 1628? Part Two of the *Discourse* suggests that at the time of the experience in the stove-heated room he had already identified four precepts by which to guide all his enquiries (6. 18). Critics of the *Discourse* wondered whether this handful of rules could really amount to a 'method'. Descartes himself had sympathy for this objection: in a comment to a correspondent about the right title for the *Discourse* he rejected the advice that he call it a treatise, on the ground that it gave notice of or announced, but did not go so far as to teach, a method. Something more like a treatise is known to have been composed by Descartes around 1628. Never finished, it was to have contained no less than thirty-six rules in three sets of a dozen each. The incomplete treatise was called *Regulae ad Directionem Ingenii* (*Rules for the Direction of the Mind*). Its version of the method is more cumbersome than the one advertised in the *Discourse*, but it is probably more faithful to the general procedure for solving problems that first occurred to Descartes.

In explaining the first twelve rules in the *Regulae*, he goes over some of the points he is supposed to have considered while meditating near Ulm in November 1619. Rule Four says that method rather than curiosity ought to guide enquiry. Commenting on this rule, Descartes dwells on the fruitfulness of known methods for settling questions in the narrowly mathematical sciences, and wonders whether they can be extended to 'disciplines in which greater obstacles tend to stifle progress' (10. 373). He decides that they can be so extended, or rather, he decides that techniques in algebra and geometry are special cases of something more general, a procedure for answering questions about numbers and figures and many other things besides. Later in his discussion of Rule Four, after hinting at the availability of a completely general method of problem solving, he actually asserts the existence of a 'universal mathematics':

> I came to see that the exclusive concern of mathematics is with questions of order or measure and that it is irrelevant whether the measure in question involves numbers, shapes, stars, sounds, or any other object whatever. This made me realize that there must be a general science which explains all the points that can be raised concerning order and measure irrespective of the subject-matter, and that this science should be termed *mathesis universalis* [universal mathematics] ... for it covers everything that entitles ... other sciences to be called branches of mathematics.

> (10. 377–8)

He goes on to say that this science surpasses the subordinate ones of geometry, astronomy, music, optics, mechanics, and others in 'unity and simplicity', and he adds that on account of its extremely high level of generality it lacks some of the difficulties that impede the special sciences.

Three rules of the *Regulae* are cited as crucial to the whole treatise (10. 392). Rule Five tells the enquirer to 'reduce complicated and obscure propositions step by step to simpler ones, and then, starting with the intuition of the simplest ones of all, try to ascend through the same steps to the knowledge of all of the rest' (10. 379). Rule Six enlarges a little on what counts as 'simple'; Rule Seven gives a technique for 'ascending', in the terminology of Rule Five, from the simplest propositions, to which a difficult question has been reduced, back through all the rest.

Descartes illustrates how these and the other rules can be correctly applied (10. 393 ff.). He starts with the question of the 'anaclastic'. This is the problem in optics of describing the line or path from which parallel rays of light, when they hit a denser medium, are deflected in such a way as to intersect at a single point. A mathematician who knows no physics, Descartes says, will be able to make only limited progress with this problem. He will discover that the line he is seeking depends on a ratio between the angles at which the rays hit the denser medium and the angles at which they are deflected. In discovering this much he will be following Rule Five, which tells an enquirer to resolve a problem by reducing it to simpler propositions, that is, propositions that have to be known for the problem to be solved. One such proposition states the ratio of the angles to one another. But this is as far as the pure mathematician can go, for, in violation of the first rule of enquiry in the *Regulae* (cf. 10. 361), the pure mathematician seeks truth only concerning numbers and figures, not concerning things in general.

A solution to the problem of the anaclastic *can* be found, but only by someone who gets beyond the ratio between the angles and sees what *that* depends upon. What the enquirer must understand is that the ratio between the angles varies with changes in the angles brought about by differences in the media that light rays pass through. And to understand these changes he has to understand other things: the way light passes through the 'subtle matter' appropriate to its transmission, the nature of the action or power of light, and the nature of a natural power in general. Understanding these last things is a matter of grasping propositions even 'simpler' than the one that states the ratio between the angles. And the 'simplest' of all these simple propositions is the one that says what a natural power is.

The nature of a natural power is what Descartes calls the most 'absolute' term in the series of considerations bearing on the problem of the anaclastic (10. 395). In general, the absolute terms of series are those that enable an enquirer to identify the 'simple' things which make unknown natures, like the nature of light, intelligible. Under Rule Six of the *Regulae* he gives some typical characteristics of absolutes:

> I call 'absolute' whatever has within it the pure and simple nature in question; that is, what is viewed as being independent, a cause, simple, universal, single, equal, similar, straight, and other qualities of that sort.

(10. 381)

The list of characteristics looks miscellaneous, until one reads further and discovers that for Descartes all soluble problems could be expressed in terms of equations between known and unknown quantities abstracted from the data relevant to a given problem. Equality gets a mention in the list of absolutes because of the use of equations in articulating relations between knowns and unknowns. 'Straight' comes in because certain equations can be expressed as straight lines in a coordinate system. Absoluteness, in the sense of what can be understood by itself and not in terms of other things, can be illustrated in the case of the anaclastic: the power of light can only be understood if a power in general is understood, but the understanding of a power in general does not depend on the understanding of a particular sort of power, like the power of light.

In the *Regulae* Descartes claims that one finds out the 'main secret' of his method when one learns that all things can be arranged serially, and that in each series there is a progression from the most to the least absolute things (10. 381). The idea is that each 'problem', each matter whose truth or falsity can be determined at all, concerns 'composite things' whose natures are combinations of 'simpler' or more readily intelligible things. Identifying the simple things is a matter of describing the composite things – light and the magnet are two of his examples – in a completely general vocabulary that abstracts only their quantitative features.

Descartes's talk of 'absolutes' depends on a theory of 'simple' and 'composite' natures: unless we are told more of that theory, we are not much helped by being let in on the 'main secret' of his method. How much of the necessary background does Descartes supply? There is something in the *Regulae* about the varieties of composition the simple natures are subject to (10. 422 ff.), and something about composition as the source of error (10. 424 ff.). There is also an enumeration of the simple natures themselves.

Descartes divides them into three classes (10. 419 ff.). First, there are the 'purely intellectual' simple natures. Descartes gives as examples knowledge, doubt, and willing. But only one problem discussed in the *Regulae* – that of determining the scope and nature of human knowledge (10. 395) – brings the simple intellectual natures fully into play. And although Descartes calls it 'the finest example' of a problem there is, and says it is the 'first . . . of all that should be examined by means of the Rules', it is in fact untypical of the questions he submits to his method. The questions or problems he concentrates on are solved with the help of the other two classes of simple natures, what he calls 'purely material' simple natures, and the simple natures 'common' to intellectual and material things.

By a 'purely material' simple nature he means, for example, such a thing as having a shape, having extension (length, depth, and breadth), or being in motion (10. 419). These are natures that belong only to material or physical things, and by knowing their relations to one another in particular types of physical object one is supposed to be able to answer some questions about the powers and qualities of physical objects in general. For example, Descartes claims it is possible to discover what the nature of sound is from the information that 'three strings A, B, C, emit the same sound; B is twice as thick as A but no longer, and is tensioned by a weight which is twice as heavy; C is twice as long as A, though not so thick, and is tensioned by a weight four times as heavy' (10. 431). These data are all to do with relations between lengths, thicknesses, and weights, imagined as measurable in units. Lengths and thicknesses are instances of simple material natures, and measurability in units is one of the 'common natures' (10. 419; cf. 10. 440, 449).

Descartes remarks that from the example of the strings and the problem of sound it can be seen how any well-understood problem, or at least any that has been sufficiently abstracted from irrelevant considerations, can be reduced to 'such a form that we are . . . dealing . . . only with certain magnitudes in general and the comparison between them' (10. 431). In some ways this deserves to be called the 'main secret' of the method in the *Regulae*. What Descartes saw was that many soluble scientific problems could seem *in*soluble because of the way they had been formulated. He thought he had found a method for solving any problem concerning number and figure, and so he made much of a procedure for translating scientific problems that were *not* ostensibly about number and figure into ones that were. With problems in physics principally in mind, he gave elaborate rules for re-expressing them in terms of arrays of points and lines (10. 450 ff.), or, where abbreviation was necessary, in equations between numbers (10. 455 ff.). Re-expressed in these ways, the problems could be reduced to a form in which relations between magnitudes could be easily observed or mechanically calculated.

Though it would have been innovation enough, he did not merely give directions for translating unclear, non-mathematical propositions into a pre-existing and clearer mathematical language: he believed that existing notations in algebra and geometry had themselves to be streamlined and unified. He recalled in the *Discourse* how, as a young man, he had been quick to see deficiencies in the traditional ways of representing mathematical problems. Geometrical analysis, he complained, was 'so closely tied to the examination of figures' that it could not exercise the intellect 'without greatly tiring the imagination' (6. 17–18). As for algebra, it was 'so confined to certain rules and

symbols that the end result [was] a confused and obscure art'
(6. 18).

To bring clarity and unity to both sciences he introduced many
notational devices that are still in use in algebra. It was Descartes who
invented the convention of representing unknowns in equations by x,
y, and z, and knowns by a, b, and c. It was Descartes who pioneered
the standard notation for the cubes and higher powers of numbers, as
well as the notation for their corresponding roots. More significantly,
because it goes beyond notation, it was Descartes who showed how
all quantities between which there existed relations expressible in
numbers could be represented in geometry by lines, and how lines,
including curves, could be represented in algebraic notation. Readers
who are familiar with representing solutions to equations by using X
and Y axes to plot coordinates are acquainted with techniques that, if
not invented by Descartes, were developed and applied by him in novel
ways in his *Geometry*.

The *Regulae* anticipated some of the innovations of the *Geometry*, at
least in outline, and, again in outline, it adapted some of the
techniques of the revamped algebra and geometry for the solution of
problems in the other sciences. Descartes had intended to show in the
last twelve rules of the *Regulae* how any problem at all, however bald
its initial formulation, could be translated into a question where the
route from known to unknown was as clear as in mathematics. He does
not seem to have composed the last dozen rules. But in the twenty-
one or so he did assemble, he arrived at a highly distinctive theory of
enquiry in general, traces of which we shall encounter in discussing
writings that came after the *Regulae*.

Chapter 5
Roaming about in the World

For nine years after he had had his vision in Germany Descartes 'did nothing', according to the *Discourse*, 'but roam about in the world . . .' (6. 28). It was a period taken up mainly with travelling outside France. Exposure to foreign customs and beliefs was supposed to help him detach himself from prejudices and errors picked up in his youth. He would gain experience and develop the sort of maturity necessary for 'the most important task of all' – that of discovering sure principles in philosophy. Or, at least, that is how the *Discourse* puts Descartes's journeys into the context of his intellectual development.

The *Discourse* says nothing about where Descartes's travels took him, or what happened along the way. It is not that sort of autobiography. It is less a record of events in the author's life than an account of the structure of the sciences, told in the form of a story of one man's progress in self-instruction. Descartes begins the story, as we have seen, by noting his dissatisfaction with his schooling, and his discovery of a method that would correct all that was wrong with it. He goes on to describe how he first applied the method with some success in mathematics, and how, before taking it further, he saw that he would have to make a detour into philosophy, which itself required him to get more experience. This much takes up two of the six parts of the *Discourse*. In later parts he describes what happened when he was at last ready to venture into philosophy: he succeeded in finding the principles he was seeking and resumed the work of bringing method to the other sciences: physics, mechanics, and finally the human sciences.

Though on the surface the *Discourse* relates things in chronological order, the real pattern of Descartes's narrative is an idealized order for teaching oneself the sciences. First there is 'logic', in the form of the four precepts of the new method, then mathematics, then philosophy, followed by physics, mechanics, medicine, and morals. Descartes's mention of his travels fits into this story not so much as a report of what happened between 1619 and 1628, but as an attempt to show within what limits he pursued the method he chose of correcting his previous beliefs. We have already seen from the *Discourse* that his procedure was to reject anything that was in the least doubtful in his learning. This approach was open to misunderstanding. Anxious to dispel any impression that in the process of removing his prejudices he was simply following in the path of the philosophical sceptics and adopting a position of destructive doubt that would leave *no* belief standing, and that would paralyse him in practical affairs, he tells in the *Discourse* how he simultaneously led the active life of a traveller *and* demolished his former opinions. He was able to do both things, he explains, because he exempted from the destructive phase of his self-instruction the maxims of a provisional moral code, the tenets of his religion, and his belief in the bindingness of his country's laws and customs. He needed to hold onto all these things if he was to be able to act effectively at the same time as he engaged in extensive self-questioning.

He compared his provisional moral code and religion to the temporary shelter someone needs to live in while his house is being demolished and rebuilt (6. 22). We must take this comparison seriously if we are not to dismiss Descartes's project of criticizing his beliefs as half-hearted. Temporary shelters are the sort of things that can be destroyed, or at least abandoned, once one has one's permanent home: Descartes's extremely anodyne moral code was similarly open to revision, criticism, even rejection, once the main structure of the sciences was erected. As for the truths of religion, these would *at first* be taken on trust, and would afterwards be proved in the course of his establishing sure principles in philosophy. But initially, according to the *Discourse*, he took his morality and his religion uncritically, and set about dismantling his other opinions.

'As I expected to be able to achieve this more readily by talking with other men than by staying shut up in the stove-heated room where I had all these thoughts, I set out on my travels again at the end of the winter [of 1619–20]' (6. 28). Descartes did make a number of journeys over the next nine years, but it was by no means a period of continuous wandering, as the *Discourse* claims, and until he settled for a time in Paris, between 1626 and 1628, it is not clear that he did in fact put his opinions to the test by 'talking with other men'. In any case, it is hard to see how Descartes could have believed that conversation would help him to correct his opinions, if he also believed that other men acted as mouthpieces for learning no less suspect than his own. Besides, he almost invariably describes the business of rooting out error as something to be conducted on one's own. This raises the question why remaining in the stove-heated room would not have been just as suitable for his purposes as returning to society. In the end one must take the various claims made in the *Discourse* about the things he did, the times he did them, and his reasons for doing them, as one would take claims made in a fable. It was as a fable that Descartes presented the book to his readers (6. 4).

Probably he did *not* leave the stove-heated room with the plan of delaying his work in the sciences. Although the *Discourse* says he had identified a task in philosophy that he needed to discharge before he could apply his method outside algebra and geometry, it is not clear that he actually postponed applying the method, or that he had cut out for himself any project in philosophy. It is possible that the need for metaphysical investigations only became clear to him in Paris some six or seven years after leaving Germany. As for putting off the application of his method outside pure mathematics, the notebook that survives from the period suggests that in 1620 the method was already being applied in Descartes's work on principles for the construction of telescopic lenses. Again, it is known that the young Descartes was haunted by the fear that he would die before he had had time to complete his life's work: it is reasonable to suppose that such a fear would have made him push on, rather than procrastinate. That he produced only unfinished work for nine years is more likely to have been the result of his trying and failing to complete something, than of a policy of holding back until his ideas had matured.

Of his travels after the crucial winter of 1619–20 little is known for certain. He probably resumed military service as a volunteer and travelled for a time with the army of the Duke of Bavaria. He may have transferred to another army in 1621 and passed through Silesia and Poland. His notebook for this period recounts a dramatic episode that occurred on a side trip Descartes and his valet made in Friesia. Sailors on a boat he had hired conspired to take his money and kill him. But Descartes overheard their scheming, drew his sword, and threatened to run them through if they tried to harm him. His would-be attackers backed down.

In 1622 Descartes returned to France, spending some time in Paris and with his relations in Brittany. A letter dated May 1622 records the sale in that year of various properties that had been given to him by his father. The proceeds spared him the need ever to earn a living. In March 1623 he set off for Italy, where he travelled for more than two years. One of his first destinations was the shrine of Our Lady of Loretto. He had made a vow to make a pilgrimage there in thanks for the vision he had experienced in 1619. He later visited Rome and Florence, making his way back to France, probably in May 1625, by way of the Alps. It is said that on his return Descartes was given the opportunity to buy the lieutenant-generalship of Châtellerault, but that he was appalled by the price and declined. In the following year, 1626, he installed himself in Paris. Except for some occasional excursions to the country, he remained there for about three years.

Chapter 6
Paris

Descartes was nearly thirty when he moved to Paris. In the six or seven years since he had left Germany he had done little to construct his wonderful science; in Paris his intellectual activity continued to be sporadic and unfocused. Part Three of the *Discourse* does not explicitly distinguish his Paris days from those spent on his travels, but there are two passages that may relate to his time in the city. In one, Descartes reports that throughout his nine years of roaming

> I continued practising the method I had prescribed for myself. Besides taking care in general to conduct all my thoughts according to its rules, I set aside some hours now and again to apply it more particularly to mathematical problems. I also applied it to certain other problems which I could put into something like mathematical form.
>
> (6. 29)

The 'mathematical problems' may have been those of duplicating the cube and trisecting the angle. Descartes's solutions, if not worked out in Paris, were shown there to the mathematicians Claude Mydorge and Sebastian Hardy. The 'certain other problems' could have been to do with the optimal curvature for certain types of lenses. He is known to have worked on theoretical and experimental optics while in Paris, sometimes in collaboration with Mydorge. He also befriended, and later tried to employ as a personal assistant, an optical instrument-maker named Ferrier.

The second passage from the *Discourse* that may concern Descartes's Paris days comes near the end of Part Three. Here Descartes notes that he had maintained a kind of neutrality in intellectual matters, having chosen, he said, to be a spectator rather than an agent in his travels, a critic of his own ideas rather than a builder of theories in his private reflections:

> Those nine years passed by . . . without my taking any side regarding the questions which are commonly debated among the learned, or beginning to search for the foundations of any philosophy more certain than the commonly accepted one. The example of many fine intellects who had previously had this project, but had not, I thought, met with success, made me imagine the difficulties to be so great that I would not have dared to embark on it so soon if I had not noticed that some people were spreading the rumour that I had already completed it.
>
> (6. 30)

He goes on to say that he had done nothing to encourage the rumour, but that once it was in circulation he tried to live up to it and find foundations for a new philosophy.

What was Descartes referring to when he wrote of 'questions which are commonly debated among the learned'? It is known that in August 1624 over a thousand people gathered in a great Paris hall to hear a public disputation of fourteen theses against Aristotle. But the debate was prevented by official edict, and later, at the request of the Sorbonne, a ban was placed on the teaching of any proposition critical of the ancient learned authorities. Criticism of Aristotle, and of the whole body of scholastic teaching that Descartes and the rest of the educated French public received, was growing more audible in the 1620s. In Paris it was welcomed by a public with a strong appetite for the irreverent and licentious in literature, and probably for subversive ideas of any kind in philosophy and theology. A long trial of perhaps the leading satirical poet of the period, Théophile de Viau, took place while Descartes was in Italy, and it was still alive in people's minds in 1626, when he moved to Paris. The trial had made a kind of hero of the poet, and probably created a great following for the risqué and uninhibited in the arts, and the *avant garde* in philosophy.

Whatever posture he adopted publicly, Descartes could not have been indifferent to criticisms of the scholastics, or to the growing influence of atheistic ideas among his educated contemporaries. He was himself disenchanted with scholastic teaching. He was also friendly with many Catholic churchmen anxious to make belief in God intellectually respectable. One of these was Marin Mersenne, a Minim friar a little older than Descartes, whose schooldays at La Flèche had overlapped with Descartes's. In 1624 and 1625 Mersenne had gone into print with book-length polemics against *libertin* impiety and atheism, on the one hand, and philosophical scepticism about the possibility of science, on the other. The book directed against the *libertins* was prompted by wide popular support for Théophile during his trial. The anti-sceptical tract sought to undercut one particular kind of criticism of scholastic teaching, according to which the physics, logic, and mathematics of the schools were bankrupt because science itself – stable, systematic knowledge – was beyond the capacities of human beings. Mersenne answered this criticism by pointing out that at any rate mathematics was within the capacities of people, and *that* deserved to be called 'science'. Descartes, as we shall see, devoted his best-known book, the *Meditations*, to the topics of both Mersenne's polemics. But that was much later.

While Descartes was in Paris he must have been aware of the controversies concerning atheism and scepticism, but probably he did not get involved. Later, after he had left Paris, Mersenne saw that he was kept abreast of further developments in the debates, especially in connection with scepticism. From the late 1620s he acted as Descartes's chief correspondent, as well as his publicist and researcher, literary agent, social secretary, and occasional scientific collaborator. Mersenne probably also helped to introduce him to local scientists and mathematicians during the Paris days. Descartes came into friendly contact with other churchmen at about this time, and was undoubtedly influenced by them. Guillaume Gibieuf, a member of the newly founded oratory in Paris, helped to form some of Descartes's opinions about the human and divine will. And it was through the intervention of Pierre Bérulle, a cardinal attached to the oratory, that Descartes promised to devote himself to the reform of philosophy.

Bérulle's intervention was prompted by an impressive speech Descartes made, when invited to give his opinion of a lecture critical of scholastic philosophy. The lecture was given by a chemist called Chandoux before an audience that included Descartes and Bérulle, at the home in Paris of the Papal Nuncio, probably in the autumn of 1627. Chandoux spoke persuasively, and got the enthusiastic applause of everyone present except Descartes. Bérulle invited Descartes to respond, which he did in a speech so brilliant that he won everyone over to his own view. While Descartes agreed with Chandoux that something was needed to take the place of scholastic philosophy, he argued that anything that replaced it would have to be guided by a method of reasoning capable of leading to certainty, not merely probable conclusions. Descartes apparently illustrated the preferred method, for in recalling his speech in a letter of 1631 he reminded someone who had been present, Étienne de Villebressieu, that 'you saw . . . two results of my fine Rule of Natural Method in the discussion which was forced on me in the presence of . . . all that great and learned company assembled at the Nuncio's palace' (1. 212). Perhaps Descartes's display started the rumour that he had discovered new foundations for philosophy.

Shortly after Chandoux's lecture, Bérulle met Descartes privately and got assurances from him that he would dedicate himself to the reform of philosophy according to the new method. Descartes kept his promise by getting down to work on the *Regulae.* The task of describing his method and applying it outside mathematics had in any case been on his agenda for a long time; thus he was not so much committing himself to a new undertaking as making a decision to carry out a long-standing plan. Still, Descartes now did something to prepare himself for serious work. Over the winter of 1627–8 he went on a retreat, leaving the fashionable Parisian circles in which he had been enjoying himself when not engaged in short bursts of scientific work. It was the beginning of a period of living mostly in seclusion, which was to start in earnest with his departure for Holland from Paris in the autumn of 1628.

Chapter 7
The Suppressed Physics

Newly returned to the country where his intellectual awakening had begun in 1618, Descartes was probably feeling the weight of other people's expectations. Not only Bérulle but many others in Paris had been struck by his talent, and they now waited to see what he would produce. Descartes had started and then abandoned some treatises in Paris (cf. 1. 135); now he set about composing a short book that he thought would be the work of no more than a few months.

He took elaborate precautions against interruption, setting up home until September 1629 in the extreme north of Holland, near Franeker. There, according to a letter he wrote in November 1630 to Mersenne (1. 177), he began 'a little treatise on metaphysics . . . in which I set out principally to prove the existence of God and of our souls when they are separate from the body, from which their immortality follows'. The little metaphysical treatise went the way of many other earlier pieces of work and was left unfinished. For a time, in May 1630, Descartes seems to have toyed with the idea of collecting what he had written in an Answer to a 'wicked book', probably favourable to atheism, that Mersenne mentioned to him in correspondence, but this plan, too, was dropped.

Another project Descartes embarked on soon after his arrival in Holland would have spared him the need to write for publication. But it depended on the collaboration of a Parisian instrument-maker, Jean Ferrier. Descartes tried hard to tempt Ferrier to come to Holland, sending him specifications for an exciting machine he had designed for cutting telescopic lenses. Had they been produced, the machine and its lenses would probably have assured Descartes's reputation early. But Ferrier could not be persuaded to move to Holland, and the scheme for making the machine was abandoned.

The third project Descartes embarked on was far more ambitious. In various forms it occupied him for the rest of his life. From 1629 he worked on a large-scale treatise that would outline a unified explanation of all natural phenomena. This work was published only after Descartes's death, the first part under the title *The World or Treatise on Light*, another part as *Treatise on Man*. While he was alive theories in physics of the sort developed in the first part of the full-length treatise were proscribed by the Church. His decision to suppress this part led to his holding back *Treatise on Man* as well. But he never abandoned his third project. The period of his working life that was not spent actually producing the large-scale treatise was taken up with making it safe to publish an expurgated version of the physics it contained.

When Descartes started to write *The World* in 1630 he did not think it would take long to produce his outline theory of nature. He planned to have the treatise ready for posting to Mersenne by the beginning of 1633. In the event it was not completed on schedule: corrections were still being made in July 1633. Worse, when it *was* finally ready for press, Descartes heard that Galileo had been condemned by the Inquisition at Rome for teaching (in his *Of the Two Great Systems of the World*) the doctrine of the earth's movement. *The World* contained a 'hypothesis' of terrestrial motion that could not easily be excised without spoiling the rest of the book. Fearful of suffering Galileo's fate, Descartes wrote to Mersenne in 1634 that he would not publish.

The World enjoyed a kind of afterlife. The whole of Part Five of the

Discourse is spent describing it and the companion work, *Treatise on Man*. Later, Descartes was to include further material from *The World* in his *Principles of Philosophy*.

From the version of the original text that survived and was published after Descartes's death, it is clear that in *The World* he stopped short of *asserting* the doctrine of terrestrial movement. Here he was helped by the literary form of the treatise. As in the *Discourse*, which appeared three years after *The World* had been suppressed, Descartes claimed only to be unfolding a fable – a story of the workings of an imaginary universe, though one that was to all appearances identical with the actual physical world.

Chapters 6 and 7 of *The World* give a description of this imaginary universe and the laws that govern it. Descartes first invites his readers to think of the universe as if from some point in an imaginary space extending away in all directions, like an ocean as viewed from some point on it far away from land. Next, one is supposed to imagine God creating an unspecified kind of matter that completely fills every part of space. The idea of a perfectly full universe was distinctively worked out in Cartesian physics. Descartes knew it offended against traditional teaching as well as common sense. It led him, for example, to postulate an insensible, subtle matter in any part of space in which nothing visible or tangible presented itself to the senses. Yet Descartes believed that it was less difficult to maintain the hypothesis of an insensible form of matter than to assert the principle of nature's abhorrence of a vacuum, which had to be invoked to explain certain phenomena if the idea of the full universe was rejected. Matter was supposed to take up all of space and its parts were supposed to be in constant motion. Motion in any part of the universe meant the instantaneous exchange of places by parcels of matter in that part of the universe. Descartes thought that in these instantaneous exchanges matter would move in circles or rings. The idea was that a moving body would not push away all other matter but only as much as was needed to fill the space it vacated and complete a circular path starting from the position of the original moving body. In *The World* this circular motion was compared with the movement of a fish deep in a pool: the sweep of the fish's fin would displace the water round it, not all the water in the pool. And the displaced water would fill up the space the fish was continuously vacating.

Descartes stipulated that the nature of the matter in his imaginary universe was to be completely intelligible; it could not be supposed to have any qualities or to assume any forms that were unclear to the intellect. In the spirit of this stipulation he assumed that his imaginary universe was devoid of

> the form of earth, fire or air, or any other more specific form, like that of wood, stone, or metal. Let us also suppose that it lacks the qualities of being hot, cold, dry or moist, light or heavy, and of having taste, smell, sound, colour, light or any other such quality in the nature of which there might be said to be something not clearly known by everyone.
>
> (11. 33)

In excluding all these things he relies on arguments with which he opens *The World*, arguments designed to show that much obscurity surrounds both common-sense ideas about forms and qualities and scholastic teaching concerning them.

After saying what matter in his imaginary universe cannot be like, he specifies the forms it does possess. It 'may be divided into as many parts having as many shapes as we can imagine, and . . . each of its parts is capable of taking on as many motions as we can conceive' (11. 34). Descartes asks his readers to assume with him that the matter he is describing is not only capable of being divided and distinguished, but that God really does divide it, and that any differences he creates in it consist of 'the diversity of the motions he gives to its parts', that is, diversity in respect of speed and direction of movement in the parts.

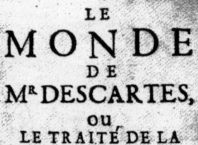

LE
MONDE
DE
Mʳ DESCARTES,
ou
LE TRAITÉ DE LA
LVMIERE
ET
DES AVTRES PRINCIPAVX
objets des Sens.

*Avec un Discours de l'Action des Corps,
& un autre des Fiévres, composez
selon les principes du même Auteur.*

À PARIS,
Chez Michel Bobin & Nicolas le Gras, au
troisiéme pillier de la grand'Salle du Palais,
à l'Esperance & à L. Couronnée.

M. DC. LXIV.
Avec Privilege du Roy.

3. Title page of Descartes's *Le Monde*, written between 1629 and 1633 but withheld from publication until 1664

Descartes goes on to describe as 'laws of nature' three ways in which matter must behave, given that it has length, depth, and breadth and parts of particular shapes, moving at different speeds. The first law states that unless collision with another part occurs, each part of matter retains the shape, size, motion, or rest it originally has (11. 38). The second law says that one part of matter can only gain as much motion through collision as is lost by the part colliding with it (11. 41). The third law says that the motion of any moving body *tends* to be rectilinear, even if in fact it is circular or curved through collision (11. 43). According to *The World*, no properties besides spatial extension and motion have to be attributed to matter in order to make sense of observed effects in the inanimate world; nor do any laws in addition to the three fundamental ones have to be specified for describing the most general effects in nature: division, deformation, and accumulation of matter through impact, and increase or decrease of motion (cf. 11. 47).

Though Descartes attributed both extension and motion to matter, only extension – three-dimensional spatial layout – was supposed to be essential. He never said that matter had to have moving parts; he held that if matter had parts distinguishable by motion, natural effects we actually do observe were to be expected. In particular, he held that if parts of matter in a vacuumless space were distinguished by varieties of circular motion (cf. 11. 19), effects would be as we observe them to be. Astronomical effects, such as the paths and speeds of the planets, were traced by Descartes to a circular motion like the action of a whirlpool in celestial matter. Thus, the planets were swept round in a vortex centred on the sun. More locally, another vortex swept the moon round the earth. The local vortex motion explained why objects on the earth's surface were not thrown off at a tangent while the earth rotated: the whirlpool action would make all surface objects gravitate towards the centre of the whirlpool (the earth's centre). Similarly, instead of being thrown off into space by their movement round the sun, the planets would gravitate towards the centre of *their* whirlpool.

These theses about planetary motion were the ones Descartes feared would offend the Inquisition at Rome. The only doctrine then approved for teaching by the Church was the one inherited by the scholastics from Aristotle. It taught that the earth was the fixed centre of the firmament. *The World* contained other claims, too, that would not have pleased officials of the Roman Catholic Church. It stipulated, for example, that once God had given matter its original motions, He would not make further interventions in the course of nature and would only sustain its operations by way of the three laws of nature. In other words, there would be no miracles to disrupt the course of nature (11. 48). A stipulation like that would have given critics quite enough to sustain a charge of impiety.

In order to make his physics acceptable he had either to revise it in a way that would conciliate the Church, or to disguise its consequences, or to erect the whole doctrine on principles that not even the most hidebound of his religious critics could object to. Eventually, in the *Meditations* and the *Principles of Philosophy*, he adopted the third of these approaches. He tried to show that scientific knowledge of the physical world depended on the existence of a mind or soul distinct from the body, a mind or soul that had to know God before it could grasp the principles of a sound physics. But in the short term he resorted to selective reporting of the contents of *The World* and to a suggestive but sketchy account of his scientific method.

Chapter 8
Three Specimens of a Method

Once he had decided not to publish his physics, the *Treatise on Man*, which Descartes had intended as a kind of tailpiece to *The World*, had also to be put on one side. It dealt with the nature of men, or the counterparts of men on the imaginary earth described by the treatise on physics. The book had a simple structure. Descartes planned to describe first 'the [human] body on its own; then the soul again on its own; and finally, how these two natures would have to be joined and united in order to constitute men who would resemble us' (11. 120).

Parts of the description of 'the body on its own' were based on an optical treatise Descartes had worked on as early as 1630. This material on optics was now dusted off, and perhaps expanded; by 1635 it had been put into a publishable form, under the title of the *Dioptrics*. Another essay, planned as early as 1629, and concerned with, among other things, 'the causes of winds and thunder' and 'the colours of the rainbow' (cf. 1. 338 ff.), was prepared under the title of the *Meteors*. Descartes intended to publish both essays as specimens of his method. A separate *Discourse* – the pseudo-autobiography mentioned earlier – would introduce the method itself and its applications in the two essays. While the *Meteors* was with the printer, probably at the end of 1636, Descartes is supposed to have composed his *Geometry* as a third example of the method. He wrote the *Discourse on Method* last. The four works were collated and published as a single work in 1637.

The literary form of the *Discourse and Essays* solved many of the problems that had previously kept Descartes from publishing. He found it difficult to write large-scale works: the chosen format made it possible to combine a number of shorter pieces into a sort of album or portfolio of his best results. He was unwilling to run the risk of offending the Church: the plan of unveiling miscellaneous specimens of his work allowed him to advertise his method without revealing its controversial applications in connection with planetary motion. Finally, he knew that admirers in Paris expected him to develop work they had seen glimpses of in the 1620s: they would not be disappointed by essays on optics, geometry, and meteorology. Descartes had collaborated with Mydorge and Mersenne in Paris on the study of refraction, and the topic was fruitfully pursued in the *Dioptrics*. The machine for cutting telescopic lenses that he had described in letters to Ferrier was also specified in the book. Problems in geometry whose solutions he had shown privately to Mydorge and Hardy in Paris were detailed in *Geometry*. Finally, the *Meteors* made public some hypotheses that Descartes seems to have formulated before starting work on *The World*, perhaps while he was in Paris.

A letter of February 1637 (1. 347) shows that Mersenne urged Descartes to publish his physics with the *Discourse* also, lest the public be kept waiting indefinitely for any more of his work. Descartes gently rejected the suggestion. He had not given up hope of publishing the physics, but he wanted the intellectual climate to be favourable, and he thought the *Discourse and Essays* would help to create the right conditions. In a covering letter attached to one of the copies he was distributing privately, he wrote that 'the whole purpose' of publishing them was to clear a path for his physics.

What did the three *Essays* contain? The *Dioptrics* took up the topics of light, vision, and artificial means of enhancing human powers of sight. It was called 'dioptrics' because it dealt with the refraction of light rather than with reflection ('catoptrics'). The nature of light had been discussed at length at the end of *The World*. In the *Dioptrics,* it occupied the first chapter. Descartes solicited comments, questions, and objections concerning all three essays: perhaps he hoped to receive a request for an elaboration of the theory of light in the *Dioptrics* so as to have a pretext for issuing material from *The World* in reply.

The opening chapter of the *Dioptrics* is almost coy when it comes to spelling out the nature of light: 'I need not attempt to say what is its true nature. It will, I think, suffice if I use two or three comparisons . . .' (6. 83). Descartes compared the action of light through transparent bodies like air with the action of resisting bodies on a blind man's stick. He compared the cause of the appearance of colours with motions a ball can acquire as it bounces off different textured surfaces. These comparisons were a way of putting over his acceptance of a form of explanation that traced all sensory appearance to contact between moving bodies. At times his comparisons were unfortunate. They committed him to holding, incorrectly, that the denser the medium a light ray is passing through, the quicker its passage. The English philosopher Hobbes and the French mathematicians Fermat and Roberval were quick to object to this implication of Descartes's optical theory, and further criticisms were made of its other suggestions concerning the nature of light.

The comparisons at the beginning of the *Dioptrics* were exact enough, nevertheless, to yield a formulation of the sine-law of refraction, which determines in general the way a light ray is deflected, according to the density of the media it passes through. (It is unclear whether Descartes discovered the law on his own, or whether he borrowed it from the Dutch scientist Snell, to whom it is usually attributed.) Later chapters of the *Dioptrics* dealt with the make-up of the eye, the perception of distance, and the best shapes and arrangements of lenses for long-range and microscopic viewing.

The *Meteors* is divided into ten discourses on a variety of topics:

terrestrial bodies, vapours and exhalations, the nature of salt, winds, clouds, rainbows, snow and hail, storms, and a few other phenomena. Apart from its theory of the rainbow, the second of the three essays is mainly remarkable for the economy and unity of its explanations. In chapter 5 of *The World*, Descartes set about constructing an imaginary world out of a type of matter to which he attributed only motion, size, shape, and specific arrangements of parts (11. 26). In the *Meteors* he proposed to explain well-defined groups of more particular phenomena on the same basis. In this he was not alone. Galileo, and later Boyle and Newton, worked with roughly the same apparatus. The *Meteors* was thus one object lesson among others in explanation by matter and motion. But Descartes tended to regard this form of explanation as his own. As he pointed out in reply to objections to the *Meteors* from Jean-Baptiste Morin, professor of the Collège de France in Paris,

> you must remember that in the whole history of Physics people have only tried to imagine some causes to explain the phenomena of nature, without hardly ever having succeeded. Compare my hypotheses with the hypotheses of others. Compare all their real qualities, their substantial forms, their elements and their other countless hypotheses with my single hypothesis that all bodies are composed of parts ... Compare the deductions I have made from my hypothesis – about vision, salt, winds, clouds, snow, thunder, the rainbow, and so on – with what others have derived from their hypotheses on the same topics!
>
> (2. 196)

He thus claimed to be doing away single-handed with the whole outmoded apparatus of scholastic physics.

The form of explanation Descartes dismissed consisted of tracing the observed properties of individual things to the natures or forms that made individuals belong to one kind rather than another. The background theory appropriate to this form of explanation assumed that nature was inherently ordered and stable, and that each kind of thing had a proper and characteristic sort of behaviour and development, owing to its nature. Thus it was proper for stones to fall towards the centre of the universe because it was the nature of stones to do this. It was the nature of celestial matter to turn regularly and eternally in place, and the nature of acorns to develop into oak trees. Except for what happened by accident to observed objects, all their behaviour was to be traced to some stable underlying nature or form, which was different for each observationally distinct type of thing. If the behaviour of a thing was not traceable to its form, then it had to be due to the stuff it was made out of, or the purpose it would fulfil when it became a properly developed specimen of its kind. Newly observed properties of substances had to be explained *ad hoc*, by adding to the qualities or forms those substances were supposed to have by nature. It was this sort of *ad hoc* explanation that was ridiculed in Molière's story of the doctor who explained opium's power of putting people to sleep by citing its hidden dormitive virtue. Descartes pointed out to a correspondent in 1642 that, without having denied or rejected these virtues or qualities in the *Meteors*, he had 'simply found them unnecessary in setting out my explanations' (7. 491).

The 'single hypothesis' he used instead was more powerful than scholastic assumptions about forms and qualities, as the *Meteors* showed. At the beginning of the book Descartes explains, by reference to the shape and arrangements of the parts of matter alone, how solid and fluid bodies can be formed. In order to explain the transmission of light, he postulates a very fine, subtle sort of matter, not accessible to the senses, but distributed among the very minute parts or 'pores' of every body, fluid and solid. This matter produces heat in proportion to the vigorousness of its agitation by the rays of the sun. Descartes cites this to explain why one feels warmer during the day than at night, and why it is warmer the closer one gets to the equator. Other hypotheses he puts forward also invoke this very fine, subtle matter. The agitation of the subtle matter in the pores of bodies, for example, causes small

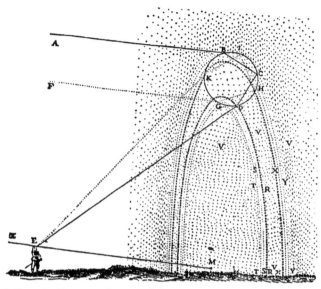

4. From the *Meteors* explanation of the rainbow

parts of those bodies to be detached and raised into the air: hence the existence of vapours. Salt is composed of long, rigid particles that do not vaporize when present in water: they are too heavy and inflexible to remain airborne. Sea water may be desalinated if passed through sand, for the particles of sand obstruct the long, rigid particles of salt while letting water particles through. These are illustrations of the phenomena systematically explained in the early 'discourses' of the *Meteors*.

Not that everything said in these parts of the book is accurate. Far from it. The 'fact' that water freezes more quickly if it is first boiled is no fact at all, and some of Descartes's 'explanations' are easily confuted by experiment. He did better when he took up the subject of the rainbow, for he was in a position to put to use his knowledge of the law of refraction to explain the circular shape of the bow, if not the order and arrangement of the colours.

When explaining the purpose served by each of his *Essays* (9B. 15), Descartes said the *Dioptrics* called attention to a beneficial art (the art of telescope making) made possible by his science, while the *Meteors* was meant to show, in respect of topics routinely dealt with by scholastic physics, how much more could be accomplished using novel hypotheses. 'Finally, in the *Geometry*, I aimed to demonstrate that I had discovered several things which had hitherto been unknown . . .' (9B. 15).

Descartes thought that his best results were to be found in the third of his essays. Some of its reforms of mathematical notation, and of the prevailing conceptions of the operations of squaring, cubing, and so on, have already been mentioned in connection with the *Regulae*. A further innovation was the description of a machine for drawing curves – curves that had previously been thought indescribable by strictly geometrical techniques, and that had been labelled 'mechanical' rather than 'geometrical' for that reason. Descartes showed that many 'mechanical' figures could in fact be assimilated to geometrical ones. He also gave a very full theory of equations, and of techniques for representing lines and figures by equations. The relation of Descartes's theory of equations to those of his predecessors became the subject of a long dispute between Descartes and other mathematicians.

It is generally agreed that Descartes made the *Geometry* and its method appear more complicated than necessary: it was a sort of insurance against the theft of his techniques. But it also prevented all but a few from being able to appreciate his reforms. Readers of the *Geometry* would certainly have been convinced that Descartes was a mathematician of genius: he succeeded, among other things, in solving for the first time a problem of the ancient geometer Pappus. But the general method Descartes was proposing in the book was kept well wrapped up. It baffled very able mathematicians, including, apparently, the one who had first proposed that Descartes should try to solve Pappus's problem.

Chapter 9
A New 'Logic'

The *Dioptrics*, *Meteors*, and *Geometry* were not free-standing treatises but advertisements for a novel method of reasoning in the sciences. Descartes believed that the method would be adequate for producing a complete physics, but he did not go to great lengths to proclaim as much. He hoped the potential of the method would be evident from his general explanation of it and from its applications in the *Essays*. He was over-optimistic. The *Essays* proved controversial and his explanation of the method struck some readers as skimpy and question-begging. As we shall see, he eventually saw the need to fill the gaps with principles from metaphysics.

The treatment of his method came in the form of a preface to the Essays called the *Discourse on the Method for Rightly Conducting the Reason and Searching for Truth in the Sciences*, better known as the *Discourse on Method*. The work was originally intended to bear a different, and slightly breathless, title: *Plan for a Universal Science Capable of Raising our Nature to its Highest Degree of Perfection*. Advised by Mersenne to call his book simply *Treatise on Method*, Descartes settled finally for 'Discourse', insisting that it was less a treatise than a simple 'notice' or 'announcement' (*avis*) of the method that would be found in the *Essays*.

This 'notice' had an unusual form. True to Descartes's aim of reaching the 'uninstructed', it was written in French, rather than Latin. It was outwardly an autobiography, but of an unspecified intellectual: the *Discourse and Essays* was published anonymously. So besides learning that the events in the author's life were being related as if they were goings-on in a fable, the reader of the *Discourse* was left guessing at the identity of the narrator. (That it was Descartes soon became widely known.) Much else was only hinted at in the *Discourse*, including, as the author himself conceded, the workings of the method the book was about. In a covering letter accompanying an advance copy of the book, Descartes said that in the *Discourse* he proposed 'a general method, which I do not really expound' (1. 368).

He was probably holding in reserve the *Regulae*, or some successor to the *Regulae*, for a full statement of the method. In the *Discourse* he did not get beyond stating four of its precepts:

> The first was never to accept anything as true if I did not have evident knowledge of its truth. That is, carefully to avoid precipitate conclusions and preconceptions, and to include nothing more in my judgements than what presented itself to my mind so clearly and distinctly that I had no occasion to doubt it.
>
> The second, to divide each of the difficulties I examined into as many parts as possible and as may be required in order to resolve them better.
>
> The third, to direct my thoughts in an orderly manner, by beginning with the simplest and most easily known objects in order to ascend little by little, step by step, to knowledge of the most complex, and by supposing some order even among objects that have no natural order of precedence.
>
> And the last, throughout to make enumerations so complete, and reviews so comprehensive, that I could be sure of leaving nothing out.
>
> (6. 18–19)

The last three precepts correspond exactly to Rules Five, Six, and Seven of the *Regulae*, which were touched on earlier (pp. 14–15). There is the same stress on the resolution of problems into components, on the primacy of the 'simple', and on comprehensive reviews of relevant data.

What about the first of the four rules? This, too, is reminiscent of the *Regulae*, Rule Two of which says that in enquiry 'we should attend only to those objects of which our minds seem capable of having certain and indubitable cognition' (10. 362). In the *Regulae* Descartes identified the relevant 'objects' with the numbers and figures of arithmetic and geometry, and demonstrations concerning them (10. 364–5). But in the *Discourse* even the demonstrations of mathematics appear to be among the things it is possible to doubt (6. 32). This raises the question of whether Descartes was working with a new standard of the clear and indubitable when he stated the first precept of his method in the *Discourse*. Did he no longer think that when people reflected on the mathematical they had before their minds the clearest and most indubitable things possible? It seems that he continued to regard the mathematical as clear and indubitable, but thought that it was only in the light of truths concerning God and the soul that the certainty of mathematics could be correctly grasped. The *Discourse* did not deny that the mathematical was clear, even very clear; rather it suggested that metaphysical things were clearer still. Read in context, then, the first rule of the *Discourse* does seem to depart from the *Regulae*, and to take for granted a revised conception of the clear and indubitable.

The four precepts of the method are announced with some fanfare in the *Discourse*. First Descartes presents them as embodying an entirely new 'logic', one that supersedes Aristotelian syllogistic (6. 17). Then he congratulates himself on replacing the old logic with so compact a set of rules. As we have already seen, this compactness in fact proved an embarrassment, calling into question Descartes's claim to have out-lined a fully fledged method. His other boast raises further problems.

What did he mean by claiming that his method constituted a new *logic*? At least this, that if one drew no conclusions in enquiry except those permitted by his precepts, those conclusions would be genuinely demonstrated or proved. The precepts constituted a new logic, because, in contrast with the Aristotelian theory of demonstration, Descartes tied the incontrovertibility of a piece of reasoning not to relations between the forms of premisses and conclusion – the composition of premisses and conclusion out of the right combinations of subjects and predicates – but to the impact the propositions made on a mind that had perfected itself sufficiently to reach ideal levels of attentiveness and controlled assent. The introduction into logic of psychological criteria of conclusiveness and truth is now often thought of as a retrograde step. But a problem closer to home is that of whether the demonstrations in the *Essays* can count as conclusive by the standards of the new logic.

The matter came up in Descartes's correspondence. Mersenne asked him whether he regarded what he had written about refraction as a demonstration. Descartes replied:

> I think it is, in so far as one can be given in this field without a previous demonstration of the principles of physics by metaphysics – that is something I hope to do some day but it has not yet been done – and so far as it is possible to demonstrate the solution to any problem of mechanics, or optics, or astronomy, or anything else which is not pure geometry or arithmetic. But to ask for geometrical demonstrations in a field within the range of physics is to ask the impossible.
>
> (2. 134)

In fact it is the *Discourse* itself that creates the expectation of demonstrations in physics that are like geometrical ones, for it speaks of the possibility that '*all* the things which fall under human knowledge are interconnected in the same way' as 'those long chains compounded of very simple and easy reasonings, which geometers customarily use' (6. 19; emphasis added).

In letters from the period following the publication of the *Discourse and Essays*, Descartes says that there is more than one kind of proof or demonstration in the sciences, and that in the *Dioptrics* and *Meteors* he had been experimenting with the sort in which hypotheses are themselves proved or demonstrated by virtue of their explanatory power (cf. 1. 558; 2. 196). It is perfectly reasonable to claim that hypotheses can be 'proved' or 'demonstrated' in this way – so long as one is not too fussy about what to call a proof or a demonstration. But Descartes puts forward a new logic, a theory that claims to say precisely, not in a rough-and-ready way, what is to count as a demonstration, and it is not clear that its precepts leave room for this sort of 'empirical' demonstration.

In order to accept many of the demonstrations given in the *Meteors*, for example, one has to accept that light acts by way of the agitation of a very subtle sort of matter distributed in the minute pores of bodies. But it is surely very far from obvious that such subtle matter exists, that terrestrial bodies have minute pores, or that light is transmitted by the subtle matter. The first rule of Descartes's logic instructs people to confine their judgements only to what is luminously clear and gives no occasion for uncertainty. This rule seems to disable the demonstrations in the *Meteors* before they get under way.

Descartes himself put his finger on the problem facing his method. The problem was that only purely mathematical reasoning could really be regarded as incontrovertible. Once reasoning relied on extramathematical assumptions, as it did in the *Meteors* or the *Dioptrics*, it lost the rigour necessary to put it beyond dispute. As we have seen, Descartes wrote to Mersenne that nothing would solve this problem except a 'demonstration of the principles of physics by metaphysics'.

He meant a demonstration in the abstract. The *Essays* already supplied a lesser form of demonstration for his principles: work in optics and meteorology that depended on them explained simply and uniformly a wide range of effects. But this was a cut below what could be hoped for, since it was at least conceivable that principles other than Descartes's would provide an equally simple and uniform explanation of the very same range of effects. Some independent argument for accepting the principles was therefore desirable.

Chapter 10
The Need for Metaphysics

Part Four of the *Discourse* outlines the argument that was meant to provide independent support for Descartes's physics. At the centre of the argument is the proposition that human beings are the creation of a supremely benevolent God, who has given us a version of His own intelligence. God has stocked the human mind with a number of 'simple' thoughts that, given His goodness, cannot possibly be false. These thoughts include all those necessary for a correct general understanding of matter, that is, for a correct physics. In Part Four of the *Discourse* Descartes describes the reasoning by which he arrives at the conclusion that God exists, that He is perfect, and that He therefore does not deceive us. Descartes's reasoning starts with the discovery of a necessary connection between his thinking and his existing, moves to the necessary objectivity of his idea of God, and finally reaches conclusions about the intellectual capacities of creatures who can trust a benevolent God not to place false simple thoughts before their minds.

Descartes was dissatisfied with the way he sketched his metaphysical reasoning in the *Discourse*. As he explained to a number of his correspondents (cf. 1. 347, 558), the work was finished in haste. Part Four of the *Discourse* was still being written after the earlier parts and two of the *Essays* had been printed, and he was under pressure from his publisher to hand in the final pages. Another source of obscurity in

Part Four, he said, was his strong reluctance to employ certain arguments he thought were necessary for making the mind receptive to metaphysical truths. To Vatier, in a letter of 22 February 1638, he wrote:

> I did not dare to go into detail about the arguments of the sceptics, nor to say everything which is necessary to *withdraw the mind from the senses*. The certainty and evidence of my kind of argument for the existence of God cannot really be known without a distinct memory of the arguments which display the uncertainty of all our knowledge of material things, and these thoughts did not seem to be suitable for inclusion in a book which I wished to be intelligible even to women while providing matter for thought for the finest minds.
>
> (1. 558)

It was, however, more than a fear of leaving his readers behind that kept him from going through the necessary arguments: he did not want to be taken for a philosophical sceptic himself. In Part Four he was content to make the point that certainty about the existence of God was *greater* than that about material things, and a condition of knowledge of material things. He did not want to deny that we could have a science of matter. But explaining all this required more than a few lines of print. In the 'notice' of his method he had to settle for a compressed and unsatisfactory version of what needed to be said.

Perhaps surprisingly, in view of how little metaphysics the *Discourse* actually contained, one of its readers, an amateur scientist and supervisor of fortifications in the French provinces called Pierre Petit, produced a whole sheaf of objections to Part Four. He took issue with Descartes's assumption that every human being had an idea of God, and he doubted that knowledge of God's existence was necessary for knowledge of anything else. The most decided atheists, Petit pointed out, knew of the existence of the earth and the sun, and a host of other things. Officially, Descartes was contemptuous of Petit's objections and did not bother to reply. But he did not forget them, and they are alluded to in the preface to the *Meditations* (7. 8). Later Descartes was to be taxed by other critics with the case of the knowledgeable atheist.

Had the *Essays* enjoyed an entirely favourable reception, there might have been no need for Descartes to improve on Part Four of the *Discourse*. It was to create a sympathetic audience for his physics that he published the *Discourse* and the *Essays*. Readers who proved friendly to his theory of refraction, or to his explanation of the rainbow, would already be partial converts to the doctrine of *The World*. But it proved harder than expected to win people over. The *Essays*, in particular the *Geometry* and the *Dioptrics*, attracted elaborate objections that Descartes was unable to answer conclusively. Throughout 1638, the year after their publication, he was fully occupied with the mathematical and scientific controversies they generated.

Meanwhile, theologians whom Descartes hoped would endorse the *Discourse and Essays* kept their distance. A number of advance copies were sent to the Jesuits at La Flèche, but with little result. One teacher there wrote to Descartes that he would have to be more explicit about his metaphysical principles before he could expect comments or objections. Copies offered to the Church authorities in Rome were accepted on condition that the *Essays* did not teach the movement of the earth. Word of Descartes's sympathy for the proscribed teaching had spread to Rome despite his suppression of *The World*, and the need for a treatise demonstrating the compatibility of Descartes's physics with the central tenets of the Catholic faith was becoming more urgent for that reason alone.

Some of the materials for the treatise were already to hand, in the form of the half-composed book on God and the soul that had been abandoned after Descartes's first nine months in Holland. It was to this abandoned book, and to his hopes of revising and finishing it, that

Descartes referred in a letter to Mersenne of 1637 in which he confessed to the shortcomings of Part Four of the *Discourse* (1. 347). In the earlier book he was supposed to have 'found how to prove metaphysical truths in a manner which is more evident than the truths of geometry'.

What method had Descartes hit upon and what did he include under the heading of 'metaphysical truths'? The method – commonly known as the Method of Doubt – has already been alluded to. It began with a resolution to take as positively false anything that seemed in the least uncertain to the enquiring mind. Whatever commanded assent in the face of the strongest efforts at rejecting it would be quite certain. In the *Meditations*, the treatise that Descartes eventually published, the resolution to reject as false anything that could possibly be doubted was put to work with the aid of some strange sceptical hypotheses. Descartes imagined himself in the grip of a powerful demon capable of controlling his thoughts and making him believe nothing but falsehoods. For the demon to be effective in his deception, it had to be beyond doubt that the demon actually produced thoughts in Descartes. *That* fact – that he had thoughts – was therefore one the demon could not deceive him about. And if the reality of his thoughts was beyond doubt, so, too, was the reality of some subject of thought, some 'I' to do the thinking. Hence the first certainty of metaphysics, that I am thinking, so I exist. This had to be true even if all one's other thoughts were in the control of a deceiving demon. And from it, Descartes argued, other metaphysical truths (about God) could be deduced.

For what he took to be the subject matter of metaphysics in general, we have to refer to the preface to the French edition of the *Principles of Philosophy*. 'The first part of philosophy', the preface says, 'is metaphysics, which contains the principles of knowledge, including the principal attributes of God, the non-material nature of our souls and all the clear and distinct notions that are in us' (9B. 14). Elsewhere he speaks of 'immaterial or metaphysical' things (9B. 10), as if metaphysics was concerned with everything that was not included in the science of matter. Descartes does not seem to have been concerned to define metaphysics very precisely, and in listing its main topics he may have been guided by what he remembered having been taught under that heading at La Flèche, as well as by the contents of treatises of friends of his that had appeared around the time he was in Paris. Jean Silhon had published a treatise in 1626 under the title *The Two Truths: One Concerning God and his Providence, the Other the Immortality of the Soul.* When Descartes published the *Meditations* on First Philosophy – 'first philosophy' and 'metaphysics' were synonymous for him – the first edition carried a subtitle apparently modelled on Silhon's: *Concerning the Existence of God and the Immortality of the Soul.*

To conciliate the Church, Descartes tried to give the impression that the *Meditations* was another defence (albeit a novel and irrefutable one) of the truths of religion against atheists. As a sort of preface to the book he published a letter he had written to the theologians of the Sorbonne, in which he presented the *Meditations* as a response to a papal call to Christian philosophers to refute the claim that the soul died with the body (7. 3–4). The titles of the six Meditations that comprised the book were contrived to accentuate its religious aura. To Mersenne he confided that the titles mention

> the things I want people mainly to notice. But I think I included many other things besides; and I may tell you, between ourselves, that these six *Meditations* contain all the foundations of my Physics. But please do not tell people, for that might make it harder for supporters of Aristotle to approve them. I hope that readers will gradually get used to my principles and recognize their truth, before they notice that they destroy the principles of Aristotle.
>
> (3. 297–8)

The metaphysical treatise, then, had a pious text but a well-disguised and far from orthodox subtext.

Chapter 11
The *Meditations*

Descartes's letters indicate that he began work on the *Meditations* in November 1639. By then he had been living in Holland for about ten years, never for very long at the same address. Accounts of this period of his life sometimes picture him as a near recluse, living with a few servants away from society, wholly occupied with experimental and theoretical work in the sciences, occasionally dabbling in philosophy. His isolation has usually been exaggerated, however. Descartes had a number of close friends, among them a famous co-worker in optical theory, Constantin Huyghens, a professor of mathematics at the University of Leyden called Franz Schooten, and, before they fell out, Beeckman. With these and other people he exchanged regular visits and letters, depending where he made his home.

The little that is known about Descartes's purely private life mostly concerns his days in Holland. Perhaps in Deventer, where a young follower of his got an academic post in 1632, Descartes met a woman called Helène, who became his lover and the mother of his illegitimate daughter. The daughter was baptized Francine on 7 August 1635. After 1635 Francine and Helène seem to have lived apart from Descartes and to have visited him at irregular intervals. He tried to conceal from outsiders their relationship to him, pretending when they came to visit that Francine was his niece. When the little girl was five, in September 1640, she was taken ill with a fever and died. Descartes called it the greatest sorrow of his life.

Francine died some months after he had finished the *Meditations*. Over the winter of 1639–40 he had taken up the abandoned 1629 work on metaphysics and had spent five months turning it into a publishable book. The need for a treatise that theologians might approve of was growing more acute. While the *Discourse and Essays* had been cautiously received at La Flèche, at the Jesuit college in Paris they met real hostility, and in the summer of 1640 Descartes began to believe that the whole Society of Jesus was ranged against him. By then he had finished writing, but had not yet published, his 'five or six sheets' of metaphysics.

What did the new book contain? Like the *Discourse*, it had a highly unusual literary form, on the one hand appropriate to its official billing as a demonstration of some truths of Christianity, but suited also, beneath the surface, to the crypto-programme of destroying the principles of Aristotle, that is, the principles at the heart of scholastic teaching in physics. Descartes's book was a diary of a fictional intellectual retreat lasting six days, conducted in something like the manner St Ignatius, in his *Spiritual Exercises*, had suggested for more usual religious retreats.

Each of the six days is given its own Meditation, the climax being reached on the third day. It is in the Third Meditation that Descartes convinces himself that his idea of God is of something real and existent. This is a turning point because of the reflections of the previous two days. In the First Meditation Descartes makes himself doubt that he has an idea of *any* really existing thing. He rejects as false all his beliefs about material objects, even his faith in the reality of simple material natures. Here he relies on the sceptical hypothesis of the demonic deceiver. In the Second Meditation he notices that to be deceived by the demon there must be a medium of deception, namely thought, and if thought, then a real thinker, himself. This reduces a little the scope of the doubt induced on the first day of his retreat. But only after establishing the existence of God does he find a basis for believing in the reality of things beyond himself and his thoughts or ideas.

God he understands to be a perfect, and therefore supremely good, being who cannot be conceived of as letting falsehoods appear evident to an attentive human mind intent on finding the truth. Error is possible when the mind's attention wanders, when it jumps to conclusions, or when it is in the grip of bad habits, like the habit of taking apparent qualities of bodies for intrinsic properties. But the mind cannot be mistaken when, taking every precaution against error, it believes in the existence of numbers or bodies, or finds undeniable the connection between being material and taking up three spatial dimensions. Since God does not constitute us so as to be deceived in what we cannot help believing, the fact that things and connections strike the mind as real counts towards their being real in fact. By the sixth day of his retreat Descartes decides that it would be folly to doubt the existence of material objects and the reality of the simple natures. He concludes that while material objects may not be in reality as they appear to the senses, their mathematical properties are clear and beyond doubt. A corollary is that mathematical physics is possible.

Descartes expected his readers to enter into the meditations he reported. He hoped that they would re-enact for themselves the reasoning by which he conjured up and then slowly dispelled his doubts. It was asking a lot, and few if any of those who first went through the book are likely to have undergone the sort of immersion in its details that he demanded. He advised readers of the First Meditation, in which he gave reasons for doubting most things unreflectingly taken as true, 'to devote months, or at least weeks, to considering the topics dealt with, before going on' (7. 130). And he estimated that it would take 'at least a few days', presumably in addition to the several months or weeks already spent on the First Meditation, to get used to distinguishing between the mental and physical in the ways required by parts of the Second

5. A representation of Descartes in the frontispiece of a 1701 edition of his works, published in Amsterdam

Meditation (7. 131). These large expenditures of time were justified, Descartes thought, by the therapeutic effect of the Meditations. If properly taken in, they would do no less than break the habit of a lifetime, the habit of taking one's beliefs about the nature of the material world and about one's own nature from one's sense-experience.

But more was demanded of readers of the *Meditations* than their time and concentration. A new method of reading had to be mastered. It was necessary in early parts of the book to take seriously claims that would be dismissed as incredible later on. Descartes remarked on this peculiarity in a reply to a set of objections to the *Meditations*: 'The analytic style of writing that I adopted there allows us from time to time to make assumptions that have not yet been thoroughly examined; and this comes out in the First Meditation, where I made many assumptions I proceeded to refute in subsequent Meditations' (7. 249). Traditionally analytic style called for a particular order of exposition or argument: any consideration introduced would either be self-explanatory or justified by what had gone before, the progression being from things that were apparent and superficial to points that were more recondite and fundamental. In the *Meditations* Descartes gave the 'analytic' style a new twist: the recondite and fundamental considerations would actually make one think twice about, or even reject, what had gone before.

Chapter 12
Doubt without Scepticism?

In expecting people to be able to follow the strange style of the *Meditations*, Descartes overestimated the capacities of even his most sympathetic readers. Central claims in the book were misinterpreted by his followers, and those in his audience who were already hostile pounced on views he had introduced only to knock down, as if they were positively asserted. A good deal is known about the early reception of the book, for comments on advance copies were solicited and published with it. Descartes himself approached two sets of theologians, in Holland and at the Sorbonne, for 'corrections', and he got Mersenne to collect comments from other churchmen, philosophers, and scientists. Eventually seven sets of 'Objections' were compiled. These and Descartes's 'Replies' to them formed a sort of huge appendix to the *Meditations* itself, when the book appeared in 1641.

Descartes was disappointed with the quality of the Objections. Sometimes he replied to them with impatience; often he complained of having been misread. Perhaps his most cutting Replies were directed against the Seventh Set of Objections, from the Jesuit Pierre Bourdin. Bourdin had been responsible for the criticism directed against the *Dioptrics* at the Jesuit College in Paris. He now took issue with, among other things, the First Meditation's very inclusive reckoning of the things it was possible to have doubts about. Did not the First

Meditation show that Descartes was a philosophical sceptic, prepared to take doubt to extremes? In reply, Descartes said that at the end of the First Meditation

> I was dealing merely with the kind of extreme doubt which, as I frequently stressed, is metaphysical and exaggerated and in no way to be transferred to practical life. It was doubt of this type to which I was referring when I said that everything that could give rise to the slightest suspicion should be regarded as a sound reason for doubt.
>
> (7. 460)

Descartes had opened the Meditation by saying that for once in his life he would purge his beliefs of everything doubtful. In order to make his criticism comprehensive without being unending, he needed to make use of possibilities that would call into question whole classes of his beliefs.

The first possibility he considered was that what seemed to be waking life might all be a dream. He observed that dreams can be as vivid as waking experience. Upon waking up we can feel astonished not to be at the place or in the circumstances we were dreaming of. In dreams we believe things that, on waking, we usually find to be false. In short, dreams can delude us. But there need be nothing in the experience of dreaming or being awake to tell us which is which. So how can we tell we are not dreaming now? If we cannot tell, then maybe the beliefs being formed in the course of our present experience are all false. And if we have always been dreaming, perhaps all the beliefs we have *ever* formed are false. All Descartes needs is the possibility that all conscious experience is dream-experience. For if we cannot rule out the possibility, we cannot take conscious experience as a reliable guide to how things really are independently of experience. No one would say, 'I dreamt it; so it must be true': how can anyone say, with any more justification, 'I saw it; so it must be true', if seeing, for all we know, is dream-experience?

Descartes used the dream hypothesis to weaken his confidence in the vast range of beliefs occasioned by sense-experience. But the dream hypothesis did not throw doubt on everything. Even if he were only dreaming that he was seated before his fire, that he had his eyes open, that he was stretching out his hands; even if there were in reality no such things as heads or hands, that would not show that there weren't in reality such things as matter, shape, number, space, time, and other 'simpler and more universal things' than heads or hands. Beliefs about these simpler and more universal things were left untouched by the dream hypothesis. Weren't these beliefs, therefore, free of all uncertainty? Descartes showed that on another hypothesis, a little more extravagant than the dream hypothesis, even these beliefs were doubtful (7. 21). His second hypothesis was that an immensely powerful and ingenious demon was devoting all his efforts to making him believe what was not true (7. 22–3).

In the Second Meditation, Descartes found that the fiction of a demon capable of deceiving him about *everything* could not be sustained. Still later, in the closing paragraphs of the *Meditations*, he said that 'the exaggerated doubts of the last few days', that is, the doubts raised by reflections on dreams and demons, 'should be dismissed as laughable' (7. 89). By referring Bourdin to the relevant passages, Descartes thought he could clear himself of charges of scepticism. But he was being misleading if he was suggesting that by the end of the book he had entirely dismissed the suggestions of the First Meditation. As far as sense-based beliefs are concerned, Descartes does *not* introduce a sceptical hypothesis only to show how ill-founded it is. It is true that he eventually withdraws the hypothesis that all experience is dream-experience, but he does not take back the message of the hypothesis, which is that sense-experience is a bad basis for conclusions about material things.

This message, fairly clear by the end of the *Meditations*, is reinforced by *The World*, which was in a way the intended sequel of the treatise on metaphysics. *The World* opens with several chapters of criticism of the common-sense view of material things – criticism of the view of the physical world that comes naturally to us, and that is based on sense-experience. Descartes first tries to disabuse the reader of the belief that his sensations or experiences are like the things that cause them. Then he devotes a whole chapter (chapter 4) to correcting 'an error that has gripped all of us since our childhood, when we came to believe that there are no bodies around us except those capable of being perceived by the senses' (10. 17). These chapters outline a *kind* of scepticism about sense-based beliefs, a scepticism about their degree of objectivity, which Descartes shows to be compatible with the possibility of natural science.

The view that enables Descartes to criticize sense-based beliefs, while at the same time holding that human beings are capable of physical science, is sometimes called *rationalism*. Descartes believed that there existed in human beings a mind or soul or reason, and that while this relied for some of its thoughts and ideas on the operation of the sense-organs, it possessed other information independently, whose content was evident 'by the light of nature alone'. It was by way of thoughts of this kind that the most elementary truths of mathematics and physics were supposed to dawn on human beings, and it was by 'deduction' from the fundamental truths that the most general effects in nature were supposed to be more objectively understood, without the distorting effects of sense-experience.

Chapter 13
The Theologians and the God of Physics

The arguments of the *Meditations* were supposed to lay foundations for physics that would be acceptable to theologians. One argument led to the conclusion that the human aptitude for physics was an aptitude of the soul. Another argument was supposed to show that the soul had to know God before it could acquire physical science. Arguments like these would help to answer influential people who claimed that the new Cartesian science was atheistic. In 1639 theses criticizing the doctrines of Descartes's *Essays* started to be submitted at the University of Utrecht, at the urging of a professor called Gisbert Voetius. Another teacher at Utrecht, Henry de Roy or Regius, took it upon himself to counter Voetius, and to act as local spokesman for the new philosophy. He was not the first advocate of Descartes's ideas at Utrecht. Another professor, Henricus Reneri, had for some time been a supporter of Descartes. It was in fact a speech in praise of Descartes at Reneri's funeral that had prompted a jealous Voetius to start his attacks. Regius succeeded Reneri as principal enthusiast for Descartes's theories and got help in formulating the case for Cartesianism from the philosopher himself. The dispute between Regius and Voetius seems to have started as a formal academic dispute, civilly conducted, but eventually it became both bitter and personal. It came to a head in 1642, when Voetius got the Academic Senate at Utrecht to condemn the 'new philosophy'.

In Descartes's mind Voetius's attack had important affinities with

Bourdin's, for it came as part of an attempt to keep the traditional curriculum of the schools from being contaminated by new ideas. Slandering Descartes as a sceptic or atheist would prevent the teaching of his physics, and neither his Catholic opponents in France nor his Protestant ones in Holland were above resorting to slander. (Voetius even reported the rumour that Descartes had fathered an illegitimate child. He was mistaken about the child's sex, however, which enabled Descartes to reply categorically that he had never had a *son* born out of wedlock.)

To get a hearing at least in French Jesuit institutions, Descartes appealed above the head of Bourdin to Father Dinet, who was in charge of the Society of Jesus for the whole of France. The letter to Dinet, which appeared as an addendum to the second edition of the *Meditations* in 1642, started with answers to Bourdin, and then went on to deal with Voetius's accusations of irreligious leanings in his science. Descartes insisted that 'there is nothing relating to religion which cannot be equally well or even better explained by my principles than can be done by means of those which are commonly accepted' (7. 581). A little later on he dismisses as half ridiculous, half vicious and false, the third reason given by the University of Utrecht for condemning his philosophy. The University Senate had charged that 'various false and absurd opinions either follow from the new philosophy or can be rashly deduced by the young – opinions which are in conflict with other disciplines and faculties and above all with orthodox theology' (7. 592).

Descartes claimed that his philosophy either left matters of orthodox theology undisturbed, or gave them better backing than was available in the 'commonly accepted' – scholastic – philosophy. But this was probably as misleading as the terse disavowal of scepticism he hoped would answer Bourdin. Though Descartes claimed in his letter to the theologians of the Sorbonne that the *Meditations* bolstered the faith (7. 2–4), there was in fact little in the book to convert unbelievers, or help Catholics who doubted, say, that virtue in this life would be rewarded in the next. The fact is that the God of the *Meditations* is a far cry from the God of Holy Scripture. As for what the *Meditations* calls the soul, that too is hard to recognize as what is saved by God's grace or punished for wrongdoing on earth. Descartes's theory of the soul is really a theory about the sort of mind that can have, independently of the senses, very general thoughts about what matter is and how it can change. Descartes's God is the being who guarantees that general thoughts about matter are true. He is a physicist's God, or, perhaps better, he is the sort of God required by an anti-sceptical philosophy of physics, one that tries to put the general laws of physics beyond doubt.

The laws of physics are put beyond doubt by the fact that they cohere well with what the metaphysics presents as the nature of matter. Or, to put it in Descartes's way, the laws are put beyond doubt by being 'deducible' from an evident theory about the nature of matter. But it takes God to vouch for the account of matter, itself, according to which what is essential to being material substance is being three-dimensionally extended, divisible, and capable of motion. The account is not put beyond doubt by the fact that it is evident or presents itself to the mind clearly and distinctly, for it has to be shown that whatever is clearly and distinctly perceived by the human mind is true. This is where Descartes resorts to an argument about God (cf. 7. 62; 8A. 17). If clear and distinct ideas could turn out to be false, the human mind could be deceived even when it had taken every precaution against error. But the mind cannot make mistakes when it does everything possible to avoid error, for then the mind would suffer from a defect that would argue for imperfection in its Maker, and its Maker – God – is perfect, without defects. The mind's clear and distinct ideas must then be true.

Descartes offers no very illuminating account of clarity and distinctness. He seems to regard as clear anything that is conspicuous to the attentive mind (8A. 21–2), while distinctness is clarity of perception sufficient to rule out confusion as to what is perceived. Confusion occurs when the mind takes as belonging to the nature of what it perceives something that does not in fact belong to its nature. When confronted by fire, for example, the confused mind can suppose that its perception of heat is part of the nature of the fire, when in fact the heat depends both on the perceiver's nature and that of an external, burning body. In general, confusion is eliminated and distinctness of perception achieved when simple natures come before the mind, and when the mind apprehends the contributions of simple natures to 'composite' things. Clear *and* distinct perception thus corresponds to what Descartes calls 'intuition' in the *Regulae*: 'the conception of a clear and attentive mind, which is so easy and distinct that there can be no room for doubt about what we are understanding' (10. 368).

In the *Meditations* Descartes invokes God to guarantee the truth of the mind's clear and distinct perceptions, but first he has to prove that God exists and that He is perfect. Sometimes this general strategy has been thought to involve Descartes in a circular argument (see e.g. 7. 214), for in order to prove that God exists, he has to use premises that are supposed to be true in virtue of their clarity and distinctness, and it is not until God's existence is proved that anyone can be sure that clear and distinct perceptions are true. The charge of circularity need not delay us, however, for difficulties remain even if Descartes is able to answer it.

Two arguments for God's existence are given in the *Meditations*. The first, which occurs in the Third Meditation, establishes that God exists by reference to the content of the idea of God, and the kind of source an idea with that content must have. The second argument, given in the Fifth Meditation, deduces God's existence from the indissolubility of the perfections, existence being one, that make up God's nature. Both arguments are extremely abstract, and trade on principles adapted from scholastic metaphysics.

In the argument of the Third Meditation the crucial principle is the following one: an idea representing a thing that belongs to a certain category must have a cause belonging to the same, or a higher category. This principle only works against the background of a hierarchy of categories – a hierarchy of types of real thing. Descartes thinks an infinite substance is more real than a finite substance, a finite substance more real than an attribute, an attribute more real than the mode in which a substance has an attribute. In the case of an idea of God, the idea represents an infinite substance, something whose category or degree of reality cannot be exceeded. According to Descartes's principle, therefore, the cause of the idea has to belong to the same category as the thing it is an idea of. More explicitly, the idea of God has to be caused by an infinite substance. But there is only one infinite substance, namely God. So, given an idea of God, God must exist to cause the idea. Descartes has an idea of God. So God must exist.

The argument has two easily identifiable weak points: its causal principle, and its assumption that there can be such a thing as an idea of God. Descartes claimed in the *Meditations* that the causal principle covering ideas derived its certainty from an even more abstract causal principle, which stipulates that effects must get their reality from causes with more reality (7. 40–1). But it is doubtful whether this principle even makes sense, since it is hard to understand talk of degrees of reality, or of an effect's getting its reality from a higher level of reality to be found in its cause. Descartes had also to answer objectors who said that the human mind could have no idea of God. He usually replied by distinguishing ideas in the relevant sense – ideas 'like images', as he confusingly put it – from pictures in the imagination. That people were unable to picture God was no argument for the impossibility of an idea of God. It was sufficient for having an idea of God in the relevant sense that one was able to latch onto one of His attributes or perfections.

In the second argument for God's existence Descartes dispensed with the causal principle, but relied heavily on the assumption that people could have an idea of God. 'Certainly, the idea of God, or a supremely perfect being, is one which I found within me just as surely as the idea of any shape or number' (7. 65). He also made use of the rule that what is clearly and distinctly perceived is true or real. Finally, he appealed to an analogy between ideas about shapes and numbers, and his idea of God. He observed that ideas of shapes or figures, like the triangle, were ideas of things he had not invented or conjured up. They were ideas of things with natures that were real independently of his thought. Equally, his idea of God was an idea of something with an independently real nature. The real nature of a triangle makes true such propositions as that the three angles of a triangle are equal to two right angles. Similarly, the real nature of God makes true such propositions as that God is omniscient, all-powerful, eternal, and so on. But while the real nature of triangles does not make it true that anything exists with the property of having its three angles equal to two right angles, the real nature of God *does* make it true that what is omniscient, all-powerful, eternal – in a word, perfect – exists. The nature of God is unique in guaranteeing the existence of something that has that nature (7. 65–6).

Many questions are raised by this line of reasoning, sometimes called the 'ontological argument' for God's existence. One question is how the so-called real nature of a triangle can exist without any triangle existing. Another question is what it means to say that being perfect involves existing. A third question is how the ontological argument can be offered as confirmation of the one presented in the Third Meditation, and yet make use of the earlier argument's corollary – that what is clearly and distinctly perceived is real. Neither argument is explained at all clearly by Descartes, and neither carries conviction.

Chapter 14
Ideas

Many arguments in the *Meditations* that are unpersuasive nevertheless command attention as vehicles for Descartes's theory of ideas. The arguments for God's existence are cases in point. When Descartes says that the imagination cannot help us to picture God, but that we can form a conception of our Maker by other means, he is articulating his theory of ideas. He is doing the same thing when he invokes the causal principle in his first argument for God's existence. The causal principle implies, among other things, that the source of an idea can be different in category from the thing an idea represents; or, in other words, that there can be a significant discrepancy between the content of ideas and their cause in reality.

Descartes never assembles all his claims about ideas in one place, or suggests a question that a would-be theory of ideas might help to answer. It is nevertheless possible to think of such a question. It can be put by asking how we are able to represent in ourselves the things that are necessary for understanding nature. Before Descartes, philosophers held that human beings were endowed with both sense and intellect, and that sense-experience brought the intellect into contact with the substances that were the topics of science. Forms determining the various kinds or species of objects studied by science were supposed to be abstractable from forms corresponding to the sensible qualities of objects: their colours, smells, tastes, and temperatures. It was by becoming acquainted with the forms corresponding to the natural kinds that the mind acquired a science of things in the physical world. Scientific understanding simply consisted of the ability to locate a thing within a system of natural kinds, a system of species and genera. To have a scientific understanding of man, for example, was to know that he belonged to the rational species of the genus animal. And the forms necessary for understanding man came via the senses. The mind was thus dependent for its scientific knowledge on sense-experience. As to how the senses got hold of the sensible forms – the colours, textures, and the like – of experienced objects, that occurred by the transmission of forms from experienced objects to the sense-organs.

In his theory of ideas Descartes collapsed the sense/intellect distinction, denied that scientific understanding depended on the operation of the sense-organs, and tried to improve on the barely intelligible doctrine that in the process of perception the forms of objects somehow travelled to the sense-organs, and were there 'abstracted' by the intellect. According to Descartes the action of bodies on the sense-organs was entirely a matter of impact, with after-effects in the nervous system and in a gland in the region of the brain called the 'pineal gland'. The impact of an object registered as different motions in the pineal gland, and these acted as a cue to a rational soul, joined with the body at the pineal gland, to have a certain type of conscious experience or 'idea'. What sort of conscious experience would depend on the pattern of motions transmitted to the pineal gland. If the experience accurately represented something, it was said to have 'objective reality'. If it was only a partially accurate representation of an object outside the mind, the experience or idea was of an object that had in it 'formally' what the idea had 'objectively'.

In the Third Meditation Descartes says that, strictly speaking, only things that exist in the mind and represent other things should be called 'ideas'. He had an idea in this sense, he explained, when 'I think

6. According to Descartes, the pineal gland in the brain is where body and mind interact. The physiological diagrams in his works show how perception and motion in the body are all controlled by this gland.

of a man, or a chimera, or the sky, or an angel, or God' (7. 37). Other non-representational things within him could also, but only loosely, be called 'ideas', such as the attitudes of willing, desiring, or judging; ideas in the strict sense, however, were 'of' things distinct from themselves. This representational character of ideas was not narrowly defined. If an idea was to be of something, there did not have to be a photographic resemblance between the idea and what it represented. Descartes said that, for an idea to be an idea of something, there had to be a 'likeness' between the idea and what it was of, but to square this with, for example, his denial that the idea of God was a mental picture, 'likeness' needs to be taken non-photographically, so to speak. 'Likeness' in the relevant sense can be a matter of a thing's satisfying or partly satisfying a description or specification one has in mind. When one thinks of the number three by thinking of an integer greater than two but less than four, one does not have a thought of the number three that 'photographically resembles' the number: one has in mind a specification that the number three *fits*. This is a way of having an idea of the number three with a 'likeness' to the number three.

The theory of ideas dispensed with the scholastic assumption of different functions for the senses and intellect. Though Descartes's rational soul may seem to be the counterpart of the scholastics' intellect, it in fact works quite differently. It does not abstract from purely sensory representations of external objects, for on Descartes's theory the senses do not represent objects at all. The senses only receive impacts from surrounding matter: it is the rational soul that represents things, even colours, textures, and temperatures. As a consequence, the properties of observed matter do not really divide up into sensory and intellectual properties. Thus it is not the case that the applehood of a nearby apple registers with the intellect while the sweetness and redness register with the senses. Instead, the fact that it is a sweet, red apple all registers with the rational soul, and with it alone. Further, the rational soul does not depend for its operation on the sense-organs, for it is only contingently connected to a body. The soul could conceivably exist without a body, as Descartes tried to show when he carried out the thought experiment of imagining himself subject to demonic deception. He found that if he took seriously the fiction of the demon, he would have to pretend he lacked senses and a body, and when he tried to conceive this lack, he succeeded, without starting to doubt that his self or soul and its thoughts were real. Hence the conceivability of an autonomously operating rational soul.

Descartes outlined his theory of sensation and the rational soul – it was actually a theory of the rational soul as both subject to sensation *and* an initiator of actions – in the *Treatise on Man*, the *Dioptics*, and his last published work, *The Passions of the Soul*. Some of his arguments against the view that all ideas came from the senses presupposed the correctness of this theory. But other arguments could be accepted even by a partisan of the scholastic theory of perception. According to the scholastic theory, the forms that entered the senses and thereafter the mind from external objects made the contents of the senses and the mind *like* the external objects: the objects, the senses, and the mind were supposed to have in them the very same forms. Descartes gave examples of ideas in the mind that could *not* be like any of the things that stimulated the senses. The idea of an omniscient, eternal, and infinite being, for example, could not be like anything the senses encountered. Nor could the general ideas of shape, number, and figure resemble the things that occasioned them, for they were general ideas and the senses were exposed only to particulars. According to Descartes, the presence in the mind of such general ideas did not need explanation by reference to external causes: his theory held that the ideas were not really separate from the power of thinking itself, and that they were present innately. Indeed, he claimed at one point that, except where they were specific in content, *all* ideas were innate (8B. 358–9). Even the idea of pain was due to an innate capacity of the rational soul to be affected by motions not in the least resembling pain itself. (Elsewhere, however, he seemed to hold that the mind manufactured or invented some of its ideas (7. 51).)

The hypothesis that the mind has innate capacities and ideas has proved fruitful in contemporary linguistics. It is a striking fact that speakers of a language are able to produce a vastly greater number of sentences than they were ever taught. It is a striking fact, too, that all known human languages have in common a good deal of grammatical structure. This suggests that part of what is grasped by the speaker of a given language is the same as what is grasped by the speaker of any other language, despite great variations in the way individuals actually come to master language, and great variations in the intellects of different people. This element that is common to different speakers may perhaps be due to capacities all speakers have, capacities that are not acquired when we learn language but that are present innately. Evidently we have here a variation on Descartes's hypothesis, a variant that is ably worked out by the American linguist Noam Chomsky, who acknowledges Descartes's influence on his own thinking.

Chapter 15
The Mind

Descartes's claim that many of our ideas are independent of sense-experience is echoed in his claim that the *mind* can be conceived of as quite complete even when it lacks a faculty of sense-perception (7. 78). According to his theory of the nature of the mind, the only capacities a mind *must* possess are purely intellectual ones and the ability to perform the kind of willing involved in judgement. No further capacities are presupposed by a grasp of the most general elements of physics and the theory covertly identifies the mind with a possessor of capacities required for an abstract science of matter.

The links between the theory of ideas, the theory of mental substance, and physics are not always obvious in Descartes's writings. His claims about the mind and the contents of the mind are best known from the *Meditations*, where the foundations for physics are laid surreptitiously. In the *Meditations*, Descartes purports to be giving a theory of the soul, not a theory of the mental capacities and ideas that put us in touch with the essence of matter. And as a theory of the soul – of what animates the human being – what is offered in the *Meditations* has a certain arbitrariness. It seems arbitrary to claim that the soul is only contingently a sensing and imagining thing but necessarily a pure finite intelligence.

This arbitrariness was not lost on the authors of the Objections to the

Meditations. They asked Descartes to justify his counting as inessential to the mind not only the capacities of sensation and imagination, but any capacity that presupposes the possession of a body. What they were querying was the sharp distinction between mind and body that has come to be known as Cartesian Dualism. According to Descartes, the mind is one sort of substance, and body another, because it is possible to form a conception of the mind and a conception of body by way of totally separate sets of clearly and distinctly perceivable attributes.

In the *Meditations* Descartes argues for his dualism twice over, once while the hypothesis of the deceiving demon is in force (Second Meditation) and again at the end of the book (Sixth Meditation), when God's existence has been established, when the demon hypothesis has been abandoned, and when the rule connecting clarity and distinctness to truth has been validated. In the Second Meditation Descartes asks what capacities belong to him, and gives a long list that includes imagination and sensation (7. 28). He then explains that it is only in a special sense that a capacity for sensation belongs to him. Sensation belongs to him, he says, only in the sense that it *seems* to him he sees, hears, touches, and so on; he cannot be assumed really to see, hear, and touch. For one cannot doubt the reality of sensations that one only *seems* to have, and in the Second Meditation Descartes counts as belonging to him only those attributes whose reality cannot be doubted (7. 24). Since he never gets beyond what he *seems* to hear, touch, and so on, he never claims that fully fledged sensation belongs to him. And though the relevant wording in the Second Meditation is unclear, it seems that when he credits himself with imagination, it is in the same attenuated sense that he credits himself with sensation. It thus turns out that no capacities that involve the body belong to him in a strict sense.

Commentators sometimes cite the Second Meditation as the source of what is really distinctive about the Cartesian philosophy of mind. It is there that Descartes announces that by nature he is a thinking thing, and it is there, too, that he explains that by 'thinking' he means any operation of the mind that, to the mind's owner, cannot be doubted to be real. To judge from the Second Meditation, this property of being indubitably real, of being immediately conscious to a self, is the defining property of the mental. One way in which this has been summarized is by saying that in Descartes's philosophy privacy is the mark of the mental.

This interpretation does not fit later parts of the *Meditations as* well as it fits the earlier, and it depicts Descartes's philosophy of mind as a by-product of the method of doubt, so that it has little to recommend it if the method of doubt turns out to be incoherent or misconceived. There is, however, another possible interpretation, which both makes the theory stand up better on its own, and gives it a central role in the *Meditations* as a whole.

To introduce the alternative interpretation, I have to mention a requirement an adequate theory of mind must satisfy. This is the requirement that it should not be too species specific. It seems obvious that a theory of the mind cannot be a theory just of the mind of man, for it is only too conceivable that creatures biologically different from ourselves could have capacities for sense-perception, memory, self-movement, reasoning, even capacities for communication, corresponding to the human versions of those capacities. Science fiction alerts us to the conceivability of extraterrestrial creatures with capacities effectively indistinguishable from our own, and science itself is revealing how sophisticated are the mental capacities of dolphins and chimpanzees. Since our concept of mind and of mental capacities extends to these creatures, an adequate theory of the mind must achieve a certain degree of biological neutrality.

Descartes meets this requirement in a particularly thoroughgoing way. He realizes that the concept of mind extends to beings other than humans, but – and this is what I take to be distinctive about his theory – his way of thinking about the mind is consciously divorced from biology, and it is less sensitive to the ways in which the capacities of lower creatures can approximate to human ones than to ways in which our capacities can exist much enhanced in superhuman beings, like angels and God. Indeed, Descartes classifies minds according to the extent of their capacities, and not by reference to the biological species of the beings who have them. Our mind is not so much human as finite; God's is not so much superhuman as infinite. And for us to have minds just *is* for us to have capacities of the same general type as God's, albeit far more limited and constrained than His own. The crucial point is that it is God's perfect or infinite mind that sets the standard for anything else's counting as a mind.

Against this background it is possible to make sense of Descartes's otherwise arbitrary distinction between purely intellectual capacities, on the one hand, and body-presupposing capacities of sense-perception and imagination, on the other. This can then be seen as a division of capacities into those we can share with God, and in virtue of which we can have something like His objective understanding of reality, and those we do not share with God and that are not necessary for objective understanding.

This interpretation fits in with a number of passages in the *Meditations* in which human beings are compared to God, passages that commentators usually neglect. In the Fourth Meditation, for example, Descartes says,

> I realize that I am, as it were, something intermediate between God and nothingness, or between supreme being and non-being: my nature is such that in so far as I was created by the supreme being there is nothing in me to enable me to go wrong or lead me astray; but in so far as I participate in nothingness or non-being, that is, in so far as I am not myself the supreme being and am lacking in countless respects, it is no wonder I make mistakes.

(7. 54)

Descartes is locating himself midway on a scale of being that reaches up to the supreme being, and while he says there is nothing wrong with him intellectually in so far as he is created by God, he implies that there is something wrong with him given that he is finite or less than supreme. A passage similar to the one just quoted, in the Third Meditation (7.51), locates the capacities of the human mind not in a natural order of species, but in an order of more and less perfect substances.

In setting up some superhuman and non-biological thing as the exemplar of mental substance, Descartes produces a theory that, to its cost, discerns minds in no non-human animals at all. (The account shocked some of his readers by implying that their household pets were mere unthinking automata.) On the other hand, and to its credit, the theory gives due weight to the limitations of the human mind. The tendency to think of the human mind as the best specimen of a mind is counteracted, and without the usual sceptical corollary. The human mind is limited, but since it is a limited version of the same sort of mind as God's, it makes sense that science should be within the powers of human beings.

Chapter 16
Body

Just as the conception of the mind without attributes that involve a body is supposed to be complete, so a conception of body that leaves out all properties that depend on a mind is supposed to be complete. The correctness of this austere conception of body, which leaves out temperature, colour, smell, felt solidity, and so on, is one of the last things Descartes establishes in the *Meditations*; it is one of the first things he tried to prove in *The World*. It is, therefore, reasonable to think of this conception of body as something designed to cement his metaphysics to his physics.

There is a parallel between the way he argues for his preferred conception of body and the way he argues for his preferred conception of mind. He starts by describing the naïve or common-sense view of each substance, proceeds to divide the properties common sense ascribes to body and mind into those that really belong to the relevant substance and those that only seem to, and then tries to explain how the properties that do not really belong can be taken for ones that do. In each case our being embodied explains the confusion of apparent with real properties. Or, to put it more informatively, we are led astray by our habit of forming conceptions of substances with the aid of the senses alone. When we take bodies to be incomplete without properties like colour, we are mistakenly objectifying their sensible qualities; when we take ourselves to be incomplete considered as pure intellects and wills, we are mistakenly jumping to conclusions on the basis of our feelings of being intermingled with or inseparable from our bodies.

The parallel between Descartes's treatment of our conceptions of mind and body even extends to the way he distributes his remarks about them in the *Meditations*. The Second Meditation contains remarks about what belongs to the self, identified as a mind or thinking thing; it also contains remarks about what belongs to a typical material thing. The Sixth Meditation largely confirms Descartes's first thoughts about what belongs to him as mind, and it also confirms some of his tentative generalizations about matter.

One such generalization, inspired by reflection on the nature of a piece of wax (7. 30), is that one cannot identify a particular object by the forms it presents to the senses. The substance freshly taken from the honeycomb has a distinctive taste, scent, texture, and so on. Yet if it is now exposed to fire, it loses all these forms and assumes others. If its identity depended on the forms, then it would have been one thing before the fire and another thing afterwards. But it is the same thing all along. What kind of thing is it, then, that persists through change in its sensible forms? Perhaps just a body, something spatially extended, flexible (capable of changing shape), and changeable (subject to different forms). If so, then what identifies it is not what the senses bring to one's notice, but what can be grasped by the intellect as belonging to body. So sensible forms are not the key to the nature of the wax, or, by extension, to the nature of any material thing.

The principal conclusion about material things drawn in the Second Meditation is negative. The makings of a positive view start to become discernible in the Third Meditation. There, in a sideline to the main argument for God's existence, Descartes considers the content of a number of different ideas he has. He takes his idea of corporeal things and says he notices that the things which I perceive very clearly and distinctly in them are very few in number. The list comprises size, or extension in length, breadth and depth; shape, which is a function of the boundaries of this extension; position, which is a relation between various items possessing shape; and motion, or change in position; to these may be added substance, duration and number.

(7. 43)

At the stage of the argument at which Descartes makes this list, the fact that something is clearly and distinctly perceived is not yet sufficient reason for thinking it real or true. It is not until the Fifth Meditation that Descartes has grounds for saying that, being clearly and distinctly perceived, 'shape, number, motion and so on' are real (7. 63–4). Even this conclusion falls short of what the Sixth Meditation establishes, which is that there really do exist material objects, things that possess shape, motion, number, and so on, independently of being thought of.

The argument for the existence of material objects (7. 78–80) is highly abstract and hard to state briefly. It runs as follows. Things that are clearly and distinctly conceivable as separate things *are* separable – by God's unlimited power. I can clearly and distinctly conceive of myself in separation from everything but thought. So – I am a thinking substance. Reflection on modes of myself as a thinking substance reveals in me a passive faculty (perception) for receiving ideas. But the passive faculty would be inert if there were not some active faculty to set it into operation. The active faculty, whatever it is, is not essential to me as a thinking thing; if it were, it would be an active faculty of mine, and would pertain to my will. The active faculty cannot pertain to my will, however, for sensory ideas are very often produced against my will. Besides, the active faculty does not presuppose thought, and any active faculty of mine would presuppose just that: all my acts of will are conscious, and this means I have thoughts about them. So the active faculty must reside in some substance different from me.

What substance this is can be inferred from the deliverances of the active faculty, namely the ideas in my imagination. These ideas must have objective reality, and must have causes with greater or equal formal reality. The only causes satisfying this constraint are bodily substance, mental substance, and God. We are not equipped by God to recognize either mental substance or God as the immediate cause of our ideas. But we *are* strongly inclined to believe that bodies produce the images. If their causes were not bodies, we would be deceived in what we cannot help thinking, and God does not constitute us so as to be liable to this kind of error. So the causes of images must belong to the category of bodily substance. So bodies exist.

Descartes infers the *existence* of bodies from the existence of sensory images. But he warns against drawing conclusions about the *nature* of bodies from the content of sensory images. When he says that from considerations about the source of his images it 'follows that corporeal things exist', he adds that

> they may not all exist in a way that exactly corresponds with my sensory grasp of them, for in many cases the grasp of the senses is very obscure and confused. But at least [corporeal things] possess all the properties which I clearly and distinctly understand, that is, all those which, viewed in general terms, are comprised within the subject matter of pure mathematics.
>
> (7. 80)

By the 'subject matter of pure mathematics' he means the 'continuous quantity' of geometry and the numerical values of variables and constants in algebra. These geometrical and numerical features of bodies are the ones they have independently of us. Other properties that appear to be intrinsic to bodies, such as colour, temperature, felt texture, and sound, are no more than complicated effects of the quantitative properties of bodies – external bodies and our own – registered in certain ways by our minds.

Quite how qualitative variety is captured by quantitative variety is never spelt out in the *Meditations*. All Descartes says is that

> from the fact that I perceive by my senses a great variety of colours, smells and tastes, as well as differences in heat, hardness and the like, I am correct in inferring that the bodies which are the source of these various sensory perceptions possess differences corresponding to them, though perhaps not resembling them.

> (7. 81)

He goes into detail in the *Treatise on Man* (11. 174 ff.), the *Dioptrics* (6. 130 ff.), and *The Principles of Philosophy* (8A. 318 ff.). The general idea is that the different colours, smells, tastes, and so on correspond to different ways in which nerves appropriate to the various sense-organs can be moved by the impact of quantitatively different external bodies.

How are motions in the body's nervous system supposed to be translated into the mind's experiences of colour, sound, smell, taste, and so on? Descartes's answer to this question is notoriously obscure. He suggests that it is by divine arrangement that the translation takes place. Apparently, no laws of nature can explain the correlation between the mind's experiences, on the one hand, and motions in the nerves and representations of external objects in the brain, on the other. The correlation is not even necessary. God could have arranged for us to have ideas of things quite other than colours, sounds, and smells on occasions of sensory stimulation (7. 88).

Why should the mind contain qualitative representations of bodies at all, if the nature of bodies is perfectly captured in quantitative terms? The question has a certain edge, for Descartes is strongly committed to all three of the following propositions: that God is no deceiver, that God arranges for us to have qualitative representations of bodies on occasions when the bodies affect the sense-organs, and, finally, that bodies do not intrinsically possess the qualities they are represented as having. Can God really be no deceiver if the ideas of bodies he makes us have do not accurately depict the bodies? Descartes's way out of the problem is to note, first, that there is nothing misleading about the ideas in themselves. They depict bodies in a particular way, but it is we who jump to the conclusion that the bodies are objectively as the ideas depict them. Second, it is beneficial for us to have qualitative representations of bodies, for it is in their qualitative aspect that bodies register as doing us good or harm. In other words, our qualitative representations have survival value, teaching us what to pursue and avoid for our own good (7. 82 ff.; 8A. 41).

Descartes's point about the usefulness of having qualitative representations of bodies applies to our own bodies as much as to external ones. We have qualitative representations of our own bodies when we experience hunger, thirst, pain, pleasure, or, differently, movement. Now these representations can mislead us, for they can incline us to believe that we are somehow intermingled with our bodies when, in fact, if Descartes is right, we are really just minds or thinking things united with bodies distinct from ourselves. Yet despite that, there is obvious survival value in our taking pain, hunger, and thirst to be sensations of ours, rather than sensations in a body that is separate from us.

Qualitative representations of bodies help us to preserve our lives, according to Descartes, and they do not *have* to hinder us in the acquisition of a science of nature. This is because qualitative representations can coexist in a mind with ideas of the simple natures of size, shape, number, place, and so on, that enable us to get a purchase on bodies independently of their qualities.

Chapter 17
The Physics made Public

The treatise on physics that Descartes planned as a sequel to his work on metaphysics did not appear as soon as he would have liked. He had hoped to start writing it in 1641, but was delayed by work on his Replies to the Objections to the *Meditations*. The year 1642 was largely taken up with answering tracts written against him and a fellow Frenchman, Samuel Desmarets, by his denouncer at Utrecht, Voetius. In one of the tracts Descartes was accused of being a philosopher in the mould of Lucillo Vanini, who had been burned at Toulouse for atheism in 1619. Vanini was held to have undermined people's faith by producing deliberately weak proofs of the existence of God: Voetius's tract accused Descartes of doing the same thing. He replied forcefully to these and other charges, in a tract of his own. Later, when renewed manuvrings by Voetius nearly led to his expulsion from Utrecht, Descartes again held his own, with a little help from highly placed friends. In the end, and despite the fact that Voetius was a local minister with great influence, Descartes successfully presented evidence to the Magistracy at Utrecht showing that Voetius had masterminded a campaign of vilification against him. The Magistracy stopped short of taking action against Voetius, whom they had shamelessly supported earlier, but in June 1645 they issued an edict forbidding the publication of anything either for or against the philosophy of Descartes.

Voetius was a Protestant. Descartes had more success with Catholic theologians. Antoine Arnauld, author of the acute Fourth Set of Objections to the *Meditations*, was an admirer even before he was asked to examine Descartes's metaphysics. Then there were the Jesuits. The efforts he had made to cultivate them when the *Discourse and Essays* was published eventually paid off, and Descartes managed to get a friendly reception for his views. Descartes had ended his letter to Dinet of 1642 (see p. 66) by indicating his wish to release parts of his philosophy that had been held back until then. He meant his physics. Dinet only wanted to see the section titles of the proposed work before giving his approval. Descartes sent these to him in 1643. At about the same time he found he had the support of another influential Jesuit, an official based in Rome called Étienne Charlet. Eventually he even made peace with Bourdin. And at least one work published by a Jesuit in 1643 drew directly, at times verbatim, from the *Dioptrics* and the *Meteors*. The time now seemed ripe for publishing the physics.

It was out of the question for Descartes simply to take the long-discarded text of *The World* off the shelf and publish that. Its doctrine of terrestrial movement was still proscribed. Its device of an imaginary universe that turns out to be just like the actual one was likely to create misunderstanding. He therefore decided to write a book that would outline his philosophy as a whole: the physics would constitute only a part of the work. The choice of a new format called for a new style. As he explained in the letter to Dinet:

> I shall not present [my views] in the same order and style which I adopted when I wrote about many matters before – namely in the Treatise [i.e. *The World*] of which I gave an outline in my *Discourse on the Method*, but instead I shall use a style more suited to the current practice in the Schools. That is, I shall deal with each topic in turn, in short articles, and shall present the topics in such an order that the proof of what comes later depends solely on what has come earlier, so that everything is connected together in a single structure.
>
> (7. 577)

He was describing a book that was at least half-written, and that was to be published under the title *The Principles of Philosophy*.

The *Principles* appeared in Latin in 1644, and was brought out in French in 1647. It fell into four parts. The first summarized the main points of Descartes's metaphysics. It was not in any sense a substitute for the *Meditations*, and the preface to the French edition directed people to the earlier book for a full statement of Descartes's first philosophy. Parts Two, Three, and Four were given over to physics. A fifth part was planned on plants and animals, and a sixth on man, but these appear not to have been completed.

There is considerable overlap between Part Two of the *Principles* and the first seven chapters of *The World*. Descartes tries to correct some preconceptions about the nature of body, goes on to give what he takes to be the correct account, and then turns to the nature of motion, the laws of nature, and some seven 'rules of impact'. The rules of impact were new with the *Principles*, and not strictly necessary for the statement of his physics. The definition of motion was also new, and calculated to put distance between Descartes and the hypothesis of terrestrial motion. According to the new definition (8A. 53), motion is simply change of place relative to local bodies regarded as at rest. Relative to one local body, the earth's atmosphere, the earth is motionless. The definition later attracted criticism from Newton on the ground that it implied, incorrectly, that particles inside a moving body were at rest while those on the surface were not.

Part Two of the *Principles* gives an account of the nature of body in the course of which Descartes argues that 'there is no real difference between space and corporeal substance' (8A. 46). The claim prepares the ground for Descartes's denial of a vacuum, for his theory of the movement of matter in circles, and for the distinction – sometimes labelled the primary/secondary quality distinction – between properties bodies do possess intrinsically, such as number and shape, and properties they do not possess intrinsically, such as colour and smell. Crucial as it is, the claim that corporeal substance and space are indistinguishable, or that matter is nothing but extension, is given a flimsy defence. Descartes identifies what is essential to matter with properties that are left over when properties bodies can be conceived of as lacking are subtracted.

It is the same method of identifying the essence of a substance that he employs for the mind, and in both cases the results are unsatisfactory. Descartes seems to suppose that if one starts with a conception of mind or of body, and then subtracts the attributes that are supposed to be non-essential, leaving enough attributes to determine some substance or other, that substance will be the same as the one he initially conceived. There are obvious difficulties for this way of thinking, some suggested by examples Descartes himself discusses. To take one of these (7. 222), suppose one starts with a conception of the human body and then subtracts from it all but the conception of something capable of picking up cups or depressing several keys of a piano simultaneously. One will still be thinking of a substance, namely a hand, but not the substance that one began by conceiving. Similarly, if one starts with a conception of a physical object, and then subtracts from it all properties but extension, then, though one may end up with a conception of something, namely space, one may not end up with a conception of body or physical object.

Apart from the purely conceptual difficulties, Descartes's physics was hard to perform calculations with. It went without a measure of resistance. It made no mention of mass. More important, it had striking drawbacks as a theory of gravity. We saw earlier, in sketching the contents of *The World*, that Descartes thought gravitation resulted from the whirlpool action of matter. The tides, the movement of the moon round the earth, and the weight of bodies on earth were all supposed to be explained by a whirlpool or vortex centred on the earth's axis. But the vortex theory did not explain the gravitation of terrestrial objects towards the earth's poles, and, when applied to celestial matter, the theory clashed with certain known facts about planetary movements. Newton, who pointed out some of these difficulties in the 1680s, proposed a mathematical theory of a universal attractive force to replace the vortex theory, and the success of this rival account did more to undermine the influence of Cartesian philosophy than any philosophical criticism it received in the seventeenth century. The part of Descartes's philosophy he held back the longest and took most care in releasing turned out to be the part that was superseded most quickly. In fact, Newton's theory probably undermined the Cartesian system more than the incompleteness of the system would have done if the physics had been permanently suppressed.

It is sometimes said that the failings of Descartes's science were bound to be acute, because it was founded on armchair speculation that he rarely bothered to test experimentally. The idea that Descartes was too fond of a priori theorizing rests in part on a misinterpretation of how the general propositions in his physics are supposed to be derived. In the *Principles* (9B. 10), as indeed in the earlier *Discourse* (6. 40), Descartes seems to suggest that there can be an uninterrupted chain of reasoning from the two principles of his metaphysics ('I am thinking, therefore I am' and 'God exists'), to the principles relating to material things given in his physics. It is clear that the metaphysical truths are arrived at independently of experiment or observation of any kind; if the principles of his physics are simply deducible from his metaphysics, then it seems that they, too, must be formulable a priori, and known to be true independently of any efforts at verification and falsification, contrary to some popular canons of scientific method.

Several observations may be made in reply to this. First, whether or not it conforms to the pattern of uninterrupted reasoning so admired by Descartes, much fruitful scientific theorizing has been conducted a priori – by thought experiment. Second, in Descartes's sense of 'deducible', the claim that certain principles are 'deducible' from others is not the claim that the principles follow logically from the others and are therefore known to be true a priori. In Descartes's use, 'deduction' and cognate expressions seem to describe an extended passage in thought from one consideration to another without doubt or unclarity setting in. Cartesian deduction does not seem to require that one consideration should actually *follow* from another in a sense explained by formal logic, for he often identifies deduction with what he calls 'enumeration', and enumeration with what leads to an answer to a 'question' or 'problem', once a question has been analysed. The reconstruction of a solution out of components of a question can be the reconstruction of words out of things, causes out of effects, sums out of numbers, substances out of properties (cf. 10. 433, 471–2). Thus 'deduction' does not always seem to assume or lend itself to a form of inference from premises to conclusion. And, as seen earlier in connection with his 'logic', his concepts of demonstration and proof straddle the a priori/a posteriori distinction.

Finally, it is just false that Descartes believed experiment and observation had no role to play in physics. While all that was 'most general' in physics was supposed to be arrived at non-experimentally, much else, in fact a host of hypotheses proposed to explain *specific* phenomena, needed to be tested by experiment and observation. The fact that so many experiments were required is cited by Descartes to explain why he personally had been unable to offer accounts of 'all the particular bodies which exist on the earth, namely minerals, plants, animals, and, most importantly, man' (9B. 17).

Chapter 18
The 'Other Sciences'

In the preface to the French edition of the *Principles* Descartes compared the whole of philosophy to a tree, whose roots are metaphysics, whose trunk is physics, and whose branches 'emerging from this trunk are all the other sciences, which may be reduced to the three principal ones, namely medicine, mechanics and morals' (9B. 14). He went on to claim that the principal benefits of philosophy were to be got from these branches, rather than from the trunk or roots (9B. 15). He said that, for a time, he had hoped the *Principles* would introduce readers to the most profitable parts of philosophy, but in the end he had found he lacked the necessary resources. His work on mechanics, medicine, and morals never reached completion, but he did make some progress with these subjects in the 1630s and late 1640s.

By 'mechanics' he seems to have meant the study of the ways in which matter composes particular kinds of bodies, including plants, animals, and the human body. Medicine was concerned with the causes of, and means of conserving, life in the human body. Morals was the study of the passions, strategies for controlling them, and ways of directing the will towards good and evil: it presupposed 'a complete knowledge of the other sciences' and was 'the ultimate level of wisdom' (9B. 14). Unlike mechanics, which seems to have depended on metaphysics only by way of physics, morals and medicine drew directly on the doctrine of mind and body outlined in the Sixth Meditation. Descartes never succeeded in giving finished accounts of either subject. In the 1630s he compiled a summary of existing medical lore, but the main source for his own medical theory seems to be the incomplete *Description of the Human Body*, which he worked on during the winter of 1647–8. For Descartes's views on ethics one has to rely on his last published work, *The Passions of the Soul* (1649), suggestive but scattered comments in his correspondence with the French ambassador to Sweden, Pierre Chanut, and his letters to Princess Elizabeth of Bohemia.

Part One of the *Passions* leads, via a complex series of definitions, and some physiological theory that is given in Descartes's earlier treatises, to a classification of the passions, and a diagnosis of the conflict between the higher and lower parts of the soul. In general, a passion is what happens to a soul as distinct from what it does. 'Perceptions or modes of knowledge' count as passions in this very general sense (11. 342). But, more narrowly taken, the phrase 'passion of the soul' covers only those perceptions 'whose effects we feel as being in the soul itself', such as joy and anger (11. 347), and that we feel characteristically as agitating the soul and disturbing it strongly.

The passions dispose us to bodily movements, producing such movements by occasioning movements of the pineal gland (11. 361). Conflicts between the natural appetites and the will (a topic Princess Elizabeth got Descartes to write about repeatedly) occur when the soul and the body occasion opposed movements in the pineal gland at the same time (11. 364). Such conflicts are properly resolved when the soul has made, and is determined to follow, 'firm and determinate judgements based on the knowledge of good and evil' (11. 367). But power over the passions is available, vicariously, even to those who have no rational self-control: people like these can be trained and guided by those in whom reason has got the upper hand.

The pursuit of virtue involves living so as never to be able to reproach oneself for failing to do what one thinks best (11. 422). Descartes described it as 'a supreme remedy' against the passions. Apparently the medical terminology is deliberately chosen, for Descartes seems to have thought of personal morality as the preservation of the health of the soul, just as medicine was for the preservation of the health of the body. Indeed, Descartes did not think just that there was a parallel between morality and medicine, but that the former was dependent on the latter. The measures Descartes favoured for controlling the passions included a properly balanced diet, exercise, and the use of drugs and 'waters'. There is, for example, an exchange of letters between Princess Elizabeth and Descartes from May and June 1645 on the advisability of taking spa waters for a dry cough and slow fever. Descartes had previously cited sadness as the cause of slow fever, and, in approving the treatment with spa water, he advised Elizabeth to combine it with a form of meditation that would free her from sad thoughts. The meditation consisted of 'imitating those who, in looking at the verdure of a wood, the colours of a flower, the flight of a bird, and such things as require no attention, convince themselves that they are not thinking of anything'.

Ethics as conceived by Descartes was not just a matter of the control of passions in individuals. It embraced the idea of the public good. In general, Descartes wrote to Elizabeth on 15 September 1645, the public interest was to be put before the private. This view was backed up by something like a metaphysical thesis: that the whole was more important than the part, the universe more important than the earth.

Chapter 19
Last Days

Descartes left Holland for Sweden in 1649. Pierre Chanut, the French ambassador in Stockholm, had been corresponding with Descartes largely on behalf of Queen Christina, who, like Princess Elizabeth, sent the philosopher questions about the passions, as well as topics in moral philosophy. To give her an indication of the theory behind the opinions he expressed in his letters, Descartes presented Christina with a copy of *The Passions of the Soul.* The book so impressed her that she asked Descartes to join her court. He hesitated, but eventually accepted the offer.

He had reason to be weary of Holland. The long feud with Voetius in Utrecht had been followed by another controversy at Leiden, once again involving followers of Descartes among the philosophers, and anti-Cartesian theologians. Descartes was accused of the heresy of pelagianism (the denial of original sin, and the assertion of the possibility of salvation without divine grace), in theses submitted by a professor called Triglandius. Revius, the principal of a theological college associated with the University of Leiden, joined in with accusations of blasphemy against Descartes. (Revius had previously been rebuffed by the philosopher after trying to convert him to Protestantism, and he seems to have harboured a grudge.) In May 1647 Descartes wrote to the university and to city officials to protest against the attacks from the theologians, and he challenged his opponents to justify their charges with passages from his writings. In the end a ruling was issued prohibiting references to Descartes in theses or lessons given by professors in Leiden. It was at this time that Descartes began to consider leaving Holland for good.

Close to the time of the publication of the French edition of the *Principles*, friends of Descartes in France tried to win him a favour from the King of France. He was awarded a pension, which he subsequently had trouble collecting, and travelled to Paris in 1648 to see whether he could get a post in the King's service. The trip was unsatisfactory: Descartes complained of attracting interest only as an exotic specimen, like an elephant or a panther (5. 329). He felt out of place in Paris, which was shaken by political troubles, and, to make things worse, Mersenne was dying. Descartes left for Holland at the end of August, and Mersenne died on 1 September. Claude Clerselier then took his place as Descartes's chief correspondent.

Descartes thus returned to Holland empty-handed, and to face fresh controversy. Regius, his ally in the dispute with Voetius, had turned against him. In 1646, against Descartes's advice, Regius had published a treatise in physics mainly containing ideas borrowed from the philosopher, as well as misrepresentations of Descartes's metaphysical views. Descartes had repudiated Regius's treatise in the preface to the French edition of the *Principles* in 1647. Regius responded in a tract, and Descartes produced a point-by-point rejoinder – *Notes Against a Certain Programme* – in 1648.

The various disappointments and disputes of the late 1640s might have been expected to make a real recluse of Descartes, by then living near Alkmaar in Egmond, but he continued to receive visitors. One of these, a young man called Frans Burman, made a record of a long philosophical conversation he had over dinner with Descartes in April 1648. Burman put to him a large number of prepared questions, which Descartes seems to have answered with remarkable directness and presence of mind.

7. Queen Christina of Sweden listening to Descartes giving an early-morning philosophy lesson – the activity which led to his premature death in 1650

In 1649 two invitations came for Descartes to join Queen Christina's court in Stockholm. Christina took advantage of Descartes's failure to find a position for himself when he returned to France in 1648, and seized the opportunity to make a prestigious addition to her entourage. The philosopher did not accept these invitations straightaway. He feared that his agreeing to go to Sweden would not look well: for one thing, he was a Catholic and could not easily join a Protestant court; for another, he did not wish to appear to be distracting Christina from affairs of state. But in the late summer of 1649 he overcame his reluctance and left for Stockholm.

He regretted his decision almost from the time he arrived. His services as a philosopher were called on rarely and at inconvenient times: Christina liked taking her lessons at five o'clock in the morning. Descartes's friend Chanut, whose company he had counted on, was away from Stockholm until December 1649. The philosopher was pressed into writing a ballet programme and then worked on a comedy about two princes who thought they were shepherds. The Swedish winter disagreed with him. He became ill and died on 11 February 1650.

Chapter 20
Descartes's Ghost

Descartes's writings were placed on the Index by the Roman Catholic Church in 1663. Complaints about his having subtracted God from the study of natural science mounted after his death, and the Jesuits, whom he had taken such pains to placate, were foremost in the drive to have his work proscribed. The condemnation of 1663 was only the first in a long series of prohibitions that culminated, in 1691, in a royal ban on the teaching of any article of Cartesian philosophy in any school in France. Some decades later, Newton's physics superseded Descartes's, and in France and elsewhere revisionary interpretations of his metaphysics, and elaborations of his logic and ethics, began to be put forward.

For the two decades or so immediately following Descartes's death 'Cartesian' became a label for anyone who aligned himself with the programme for a 'complete philosophy' that had been outlined in the preface to the French edition of *The Principles of Philosophy*. Descartes had said in the preface that Parts Two, Three, and Four of the *Principles* contained all that was most general in physics (9B. 16), but that more was needed to state a complete science of material substance. The *Principles* included formulations of the laws of nature, a cosmological theory, or account of the make-up and generation of the physical universe, and an explanation of the 'elements' or bodies most commonly found on the earth, and their qualities. But concerning 'particular bodies', namely minerals, plants, animals, and, most importantly, man, much remained to be said.

To supply this missing material, Descartes said, observations and experiments were needed that were both too numerous and too expensive for one man to perform (9B. 17). These were the observations and experiments that the earliest of the 'Cartesians' undertook to carry out. Working with the laws of motion as stated in Part Two of the *Principles*, the theory of vortices or whirlpools of matter in Part Three, and the doctrine of the subtle matter in Parts Three and Four, scientists such as Jacques Rohault and Pierre Sylvain in France, and Johannes Clauberg in Holland and Germany, tried, in effect, to supply the missing pieces of Descartes's physics. Their research programme petered out when serious anomalies in the Cartesian theory of gravity, and of planetary motion and position, were corrected by Newton, whose radically different theory took as irreducible a notion of force (universal attractive force) that Descartes could not accommodate.

In the description of how to instruct oneself in philosophy that he gave in the preface to the French edition of the *Principles*, Descartes said that before confronting physics one should immerse oneself in metaphysics, and that before approaching metaphysics one should practise logic:

> I do not mean the logic of the schools, for this is strictly speaking nothing but a dialectic which teaches ways of expounding to others what one already knows or even of holding forth without judgement about things one does not know . . . I mean the kind of logic which teaches us to direct our reason with a view to discovering the truths of which we are ignorant.
>
> (9B. 13–14)

We have already gained an impression of this 'logic' from earlier comments on the *Regulae* and the four precepts stated in Part Two of the *Discourse*. After Descartes's death, in 1664, Antoine Arnauld and Pierre

8. The skull of Descartes, preserved in the Musée de l'Homme in Paris

Nicole issued *La Logique, ou l'art de penser* (*Logic, or the Art of Thinking*), in which the *Regulae,* not published during Descartes's lifetime but found among his papers at his death, was adapted and enlarged upon. Arnauld and Nicole were not the only or even the first of Descartes's followers to try to spell out the 'new' logic. Johannes Clauberg, already mentioned in connection with the Cartesian movement in physics, tried to do the same thing.

Works by other philosophers, scientists, and theologians of the period can also be read as contributions to the programme Descartes was unable to complete. Arnold Geulincx, a Flemish philosopher, produced a treatise on ethics along Cartesian lines in 1655. There is, too, a long list of philosophers, Geulincx included, who attempted to clear up the many difficulties in Descartes's metaphysics. Problems concerning ideas, and the relation between mind and body, preoccupied the earlier commentators, as did the Cartesian theory of causality, and the metaphysical theory of the relation between substance and attribute.

Arnauld, Nicholas Malebranche, and Simon Foucher were leading figures in the controversies concerning metaphysics soon after Descartes's death. Leibniz and Spinoza elaborated systems that were intended to be, in some ways, more thoroughly Cartesian – more rigorously deductive – even than Descartes's own. In Britain, John Locke reacted against the innatism of Cartesian epistemology, but retained a theory of ideas. George Berkeley and David Hume, influenced by Malebranche, joined in the criticism and revision of the Cartesian theory of two substances, and of a causally efficacious material substance. The work of all these writers is much closer than that of Cartesian physicists and moralists to studies of Descartes today, for the Descartes who still haunts people is the ghost of a philosopher, not of a physicist, doctor, or teacher of ethics.

Except for those who applaud the Cartesian spirit of innatism in linguistics, philosophers in the English-speaking world are nowadays mostly agreed on the need to lay Descartes's ghost. It says a lot for the power of Cartesian philosophy that the activity of interring it still goes on. Philosophers continue to express elaborate disagreement with Descartes's theory of ideas, his dualism, his view that science must proceed from self-evident principles, and his belief that considerations about knowledge lie at the centre of philosophy. There is a system in these doctrines, and this helps to explain their staying power. They are all arrived at in the course of discharging a single task, namely that of showing that a mathematical understanding of the physical world is more objective than one suggested by the senses, and that the human intellect is capable of forming this more objective conception. No doubt Descartes's way of establishing these things is full of misconceptions. Generations of critics have proved as much. But the criticism would not have endured if philosophers were not still captivated by Descartes's task. They still are captivated. They still are inclined to argue about the types of subject matter it is possible to have an increasingly objective understanding of. What lends sense to these arguments is the clear picture we now have of what it is like to understand the *material* world better and better. An early version of this picture is due to Descartes. It is what makes it so difficult to lay his ghost.

Further Reading

Descartes's Own Writings

The two-volume selection by Cottingham, Stoothoff, and Murdoch (see under Texts and Translations) is the most satisfactory collection of Descartes's writings in English. Individual philosophical texts by Descartes are also widely available in paperback editions published by Penguin, Everyman, Mentor, and Nelson. A particularly useful translation by Stephen Voss of *The Passions of the Soul* (Indianapolis, 1989) can also be mentioned in this connection. The selection of Descartes's enormous correspondence translated by Anthony Kenny (see under Texts and Translations, p. ix) has now been corrected, enlarged, and incorporated as a third volume into the Cottingham, Stoothoff, and Murdoch edition of Descartes's writings. Further correspondence, on psychology and ethics, has been translated by John Blom (see below). Also of interest is Descartes's *Conversation with Burman*, edited and translated by John Cottingham (Oxford: Clarendon Press, 1976).

Descartes's scientific writings are usually excerpted rather than printed complete. The selections given in Cottingharn *et al.* should meet the needs of the general reader. For the *Discourse and Essays* in its entirety, see the English translation by Paul Olscamp (Indianapolis: Bobbs-Merrill, 1965). See also T. S. Hall (trans.), *Treatise of Man* (Cambridge, Mass.: Harvard University Press, 1972), and the translation of *The Principles of Philosophy* published by Reidel in 1984.

In French, besides the Adam and Tannery, there is an edition of Descartes's writings by Alquié (Paris: Gamier, 1963–73).

Biographies

The first biography of Descartes was Adrien Baillet's *La Vie de Monsieur Descartes*, published in 1691 (Paris: La Table Ronde, 1946), recently reprinted by Slatkine Reprints (Geneva, 1970). Modern accounts of Descartes's life, which at times correct Baillet, include Charles Adam, *Vie et Œuvres de Descartes* (1910; AT, vol. 12), on which I have relied heavily, and, in English, Jack Vrooman, *René Descartes: A Biography* (New York: Putnam, 1970). Much more recent is Stephen Gaukroger, *Descartes: An Intellectual Biography* (Oxford: Clarendon Press, 1995), which has a very full treatment of Descartes's scientific writings.

Descartes's Science

Apart from Gaukroger's biography of Descartes, one of the few recent books to cover Descartes's philosophy *and* science is Daniel Garber's excellent *Descartes' Metaphysical Physics* (Chicago: University of Chicago Press, 1992). Considerably older but still worth consulting is Jonathan Rée, *Descartes* (London: Allen Lane, 1974). More on Descartes's philosophy and science can be found in Desmond Clarke, *Descartes' Philosophy of Science* (Manchester: Manchester University Press, 1982), and the collection of papers edited by Stephen Gaukroger, *Descartes: Philosophy, Mathematics, and Physics* (Brighton: Harvester, 1980).

Descartes's science is considered in some depth in J. F. Scott, *The Scientific Work of René Descartes* (London: Taylor and Francis, 1952). Also useful is the chapter on Descartes in volume 7 of Lynn Thorndike, *History of Magic and Experimental Science* (New York: Columbia University Press, 1958).

For a more general survey, see Gerd Buchdahl, *Metaphysics and the Philosophy of Science: The Classical Origins – Descartes to Kant* (Oxford: Blackwell, 1969).

Philosophy

Among the many good books on Descartes's philosophy, I mention: Anthony Kenny, *Descartes: A Study of his Philosophy* (New York: Random House, 1968); Harry Frankfurt, *Demons, Dreamers and Madmen: The Defence of Reason in Descartes's Metaphysics* (Indianapolis: Bobbs-Merrill, 1970); Bernard Williams, *Descartes: The Project of Pure Enquiry* (Harmondsworth: Penguin, 1978); E. M. Curley, *Descartes against the Sceptics* (Oxford: Blackwell, 1978); Margaret Wilson, *Descartes* (London: Routledge and Kegan Paul, 1978); John Cottingham, *Descartes* (Oxford: Blackwell, 1986).

Recent collections of articles on Descartes's philosophy include John Cottingham (ed.), *The Cambridge Companion to Descartes* (Cambridge: Cambridge University Press, 1992), Stephen Voss, *Essays on the Philosophy and Science of Descartes* (Oxford: Oxford University Press, 1993), and John Cottingham (ed.), *Reason, Will and Sensation: Essays on Descartes's Metaphysics* (Oxford: Clarendon Press, 1994). A collection of articles on the Objectors to the *Meditations* edited by Roger Ariew and Marjorie Grene (Chicago: University of Chicago Press, 1995) includes contributions from leading French Descartes scholars.

Ethics and Medical Writings

Texts, including letters, relevant to a study of what Descartes calls 'morals', are assembled in John Blom (trans.), *Descartes: His Moral Philosophy and Psychology* (Hassocks: Harvester, 1978).

Descartes's medical writings are discussed and interpreted in Richard Carter, *Descartes's Medical Philosophy* (Baltimore: Johns Hopkins University Press, 1978).

Influence of Descartes after his Death

On Cartesianism in philosophy after Descartes's death, see Norman Kemp Smith, *Studies in the Cartesian Philosophy* (London: Macmillan,

1902), and Richard Watson, *The Downfall of Cartesianism 1673–1712* (The Hague: Martinus Nijhoff, 1966).

The influence of Cartesian innatism in linguistics is discussed in Part Three of S. Stich (ed.), *Innate Ideas* (Berkeley and Los Angeles: University of California Press, 1975).

For an indication of reactions against Descartes in latter-day philosophy, see Rée (cited above), and Richard Rorty, *Philosophy and the Mirror of Nature* (Oxford: Blackwell, 1980).

Index